Stories & Jokes of Mormon Folks

Happy Birthday
Coral,
this may be the
year we need to
laugh!
Love Always
Chris

Stories & Jokes of Mormon Folks

A collection by

Bruce E. Dana

spring creek
BOOK COMPANY

Provo, Utah

© 2007 Bruce E. Dana
All Rights Reserved.

ISBN 10: 1-932898-67-0
ISBN 13: 978-1-932898-67-5
e. 1

Published by:
Spring Creek Book Company
P.O. Box 50355
Provo, Utah 84605-0355

www.springcreekbooks.com

Cover design © Spring Creek Book Company
Cover design by Nicole Cunningham

Printed in the United States of America
10 9 8 7 6 5 4 3 2 1
Printed on acid-free paper

Library of Congress Control Number: 2006935536

ACKNOWLEDGMENTS

As always, I am indebted to my wife, Brenda, for allowing me valuable time to research and write. I appreciate all of my family members—whose numbers happily keep increasing—for their constant love and support.

I am grateful for all who contributed and granted me permission to use their humor in this book. In addition, I am thankful to my publisher, Spring Creek Book Company, for their willingness to publish this work.

TABLE OF CONTENTS

INTRODUCTION

A good sense of humor is a characteristic of a well-balanced individual. The gospel of Jesus Christ is a happy, pleasant gospel. This collection of humor is not intended to make light of gospel teachings or its practices, but to add a little humor and sparkle to the life of the reader.

With that in mind, I do realize that a joke or story that is considered humorous to one individual will not necessarily be to another.

The jokes and stories in this work have been collected from various sources over a period of years and are based solely upon my own understanding and personality.

I have strived to give credit to those individuals who have shared their humor with me. However, if no name is written, it is from Mr. Anonymous.

Bruce E. Dana
October 2006

ACTION OF A MEMBER

As with all mankind, every member of the Church performs an action in this life, either by words or deeds, or a combination of the two. The following are the lighter side of an action of some members of the Church:

A man was being tailgated by a woman in a car on a busy boulevard. Suddenly, the light turned yellow, just in front of him. He did the right thing, stopping his car at the crosswalk, even though he could have beaten the red light by accelerating through the intersection.

The woman slammed on her brakes and leaned on the horn. She opened her window, stuck her hand out and made a gesture, all the while screaming in frustration as she missed her chance to get through the intersection. As she was still in mid-rant, she heard a tap on her car window and looked up into the face of a very serious police officer.

The officer ordered her to exit her car with her hands up. He took her to the police station where she was searched, fingerprinted, photographed, and placed in a cell.

After a couple of hours, a policeman approached the cell and opened the door. This woman was escorted back to the booking desk where the arresting officer was waiting with her personal belongings. He said, "I'm very sorry for this mistake. You see, I pulled up behind your car while you were blowing your horn, giving a hand gesture, and cussing a blue streak at the man in front of you.

"I noticed the 'Choose the Right' license plate holder, the 'Families are Forever' bumper sticker, the 'Follow Me to Sunday School' bumper sticker, and the chrome-plated Angel Moroni emblem on the trunk—Naturally, I assumed you had stolen the car!"

At times, we are quick to judge people. One evening, a senior home teaching companion learned a great lesson. This older Brother knocked on the door of one of his home teaching families, but received no response.

After knocking several times, he looked at his youthful companion and said he was annoyed because he could hear the vacuum going and knew that the mother of the family was inside. Irritated that they would have to return again another evening, this senior companion wrote a short scripture and slid it under the screen door.

The following was written on his note:

Revelations 3:20
"Behold, I stand at the door, and knock:
"if any man hear my voice, and open the door,
"I will come in to him . . . ."

The next Sunday, when this senior companion met the sister at Church, she acted somewhat embarrassed. And well she should be, he thought. It is difficult to make an extra appointment, and he believed that his time was valuable. When this Brother tried to talk to this sister, she quietly slipped him this note: "Please read Genesis Chapter 3 verse 10." This Brother could hardly wait to look up in his scriptures to see what kind of an apology this sister could possibly give for being what he thought was rude. He opened his scriptures and read:

Genesis 3:10
". . . I heard thy voice in the garden,
"and I was afraid, because I was naked;
"and I hid myself."

A young boy entered his Bishop's office and put a piggy bank of money on the desk. The Bishop said, "Thank you. This must be for your tithing?"
"No," the lad replied.
The Bishop asked, "Is it for the fast offering fund—to help the poor and the needy?"
"No," answered the boy.
The Bishop then asked, "Is it for the missionary fund—to help the full-time missionaries?"
"No," said the child.

Perplexed, the Bishop asked, "Who is it for?"

The boy leaned over the desk and innocently answered, "I heard my mother and dad speaking and they said you were the poorest Bishop we've ever had."

One Sunday morning a Bishop noticed that a young boy, whose family moved in his ward boundaries the week previous, was staring at the plaque that hung in the foyer of the stake center. The lad, age 8, had been staring at the plaque for some time, so the Bishop walked over and stood beside him and said, "Good morning; I'm Bishop Allen."

"Good morning," the boy replied, not taking his eyes off of the plaque. The boy then asked, "What is this?"

"It is a plaque listing the names of members in our stake who have died in the service."

The boy innocently asked, "Which one, Bishop, the regular Sunday service or the Fast Sunday service?"

A true, paraphrased story:

One day Brother Barlow L. Packer needed a radio knob for his Volkswagen bug car and he went to the dealership parts department to buy one. He was about sixth in line at the parts department, where a clerk was trying to wait on people and answer the telephone at the same time.

He stood there for about 10 minutes and observed that the same thing happened time and again. The telephone would ring and the parts clerk would pick it up and answer, "Parts Department." The clerk would listen for a minute and then say, "Let me check." He would leave the counter and check for the part, then come back and pick up the telephone and say, "Yes, we have it." Sometimes, he would look up the price of the part. This clerk would hang up the phone and ask the person in line what part he needed again, and then be distracted by the ringing of the telephone.

Those people standing in line became frustrated, grumbling about the service. Brother Barlow began shifting his feet and checking his watch.

The clerk was doing his best, but couldn't do two jobs at the same time. For some reason, he felt that the ringing telephone was more important than helping the people who were standing in line.

Brother Barlow could see that he was in for a long wait. Looking around he noticed a public pay phone near by. He left his place in line and went to the pay phone, looked up the number of the Parts Department, and dialed the number.

The telephone on the counter rang and the clerk picked up the phone.

"This is the Parts Department."

"Do you have a radio on-off knob for a '69 VW bug?"

"Let me check."

Before the clerk could lay the phone down on the counter, Brother Barlow said, "If you do, will you please bring it to the counter? I'll be right there, and you won't have to look for it again."

The clerk put down the telephone and in a minute or two he came to counter with the part in his hand. Before he could pick up the telephone, Brother Barlow walked from the line and approached the counter and said, "I'm the guy who just called about this VW knob."

He said that he'll never forget the look on the clerk's face when he figured out what had happened. Brother Barlow said to him sympathetically, "It is difficult doing this all alone, isn't it?"

"Yes," said the clerk.

"Why not leave the telephone off the hook for a few minutes."

The other people in line all exclaimed, "Yes."

The clerk suddenly realized that a caller who was getting a busy signal would call back shortly.

(The Soft Reply, Bookcraft, 1997, pp. 31-32)

ADAM AND EVE

The Lord said, "And the first man of all men have I called Adam, which is many." [Moses 1:34]

Adam was placed on this earth as the first of the human family and given a name which signifies "many" as pertaining to the greatness of the posterity which should flow from him.

The first woman of all women was named Eve, who is a daughter of God; her name signifying "mother of all living." Eve was the wife of Adam, and she was placed on this earth in the same manner as was Adam.

God the Father gave them a commandment to multiply and replenish the earth, and not to eat the fruit of the tree of knowledge of good and evil. Having agency, and being tempted of Lucifer, Eve first ate the forbidden fruit, and then Adam.

Because of their transgression, Adam and Eve fell both spiritually and temporally, and the Lord had them driven out of the Garden of Eden.

Regarding the forbidden fruit, the Lord has not revealed what type it was. Whether correct or not, many people believe it was an apple.

Latter-day revelation tells us that Adam and Eve

had many sons and daughters, including the famous duo, Cain and Abel.

The following are the lighter side of the story of Adam and Eve:

God the Father knew that Adam was all alone in the Garden of Eden, so He decided to create a companion for this first man of all men.

God visited the earth and said, "Adam, you are my greatest creation; therefore, I am going to create for you a helpmate: a beautiful, intelligent woman, who will adore you and take care of you. She will be your wife and the mother of your children."

Adam replied excitedly, "That is wonderful."

Teasing, the Father said, "All it will cost you is an arm and a leg."

Thinking that Father was serious, Adam timidly replied, "What can I get for a rib?"

The following questions and answers about Adam and Eve have been told for years, and will be enjoyed by younger children:

Question: At what time of day was Adam created?
Answer: A little before Eve.

Question: Did Eve ever have a date with Adam?
Answer: No; it was an apple.

Question: What type of coat did Adam and Eve
      wear?
Answer: Bare skin.

Question: Where is the first math problem mentioned
      in the Bible?
Answer: In Genesis—when God the Father told
      Adam and Eve to go forth and multiply.

Question: What was the phone number for the
      Garden of Eden?
Answer: Adam 8-1-2.

Question: How did Adam and Eve feel when they
      were driven from the Garden of Eden?
Answer: They were put out.

Question: What is one of the things that Adam
      and Eve did after they were driven from the
      Garden of Eden?
Answer: They raised a little Cain.

Question: How do we know that Adam had sugar?
Answer: He raised Cain.

Question: How long did Cain dislike his brother?
Answer: As long as he was Abel.

Question: When was the longest day in the Garden
of Eden?
Answer: When there was no Eve.

A short poem about Adam's day:

Adam had his troubles no doubt,
In days of yore;
But no one said out loud,
when he had told a yarn—
"I've heard that one before."

After telling the story of Adam and Eve eating the
forbidden fruit, a grandmother asked her grandson
what the pair had done wrong.

He thought briefly and answered, "They didn't
wash their hands before eating."

—Sally Dickman

The story of Adam and Eve was carefully explained in a Primary class. Following the story, the children were asked to draw a picture that would illustrate this story.

Tommy was most interested and drew a picture of a car with three people in it. In the front seat, behind the steering wheel, was a man; in the back seat sat a man and a woman.

The teacher was curious as to know how this picture illustrated the lesson, so she asked Tommy to explain his drawing.

He replied, "This is God driving Adam and Eve out of the Garden!"

Adam, with his young sons, Cain and Abel were one day working in the field. It was hot and dusty, and the work was hard. Desiring a break, the sons convinced their father to climb a small hill to find a cool breeze.

After climbing the hill, the boys saw for the first time the Garden of Eden at a distance. It was beautiful, with tall green hills, fruits and melons, and a waterfall of clear water. Enthusiastically the boys asked their father about this place. Adam explained that it was a choice garden where no weeds grew and fruits and melons grew without needing any care. Cain and Abel curiously asked, "Why don't we live there?"

Not telling the full story about eating the forbidden fruit, Adam smiled and answered, "I and your mother used to live there, until your mother ate us out of house and home."

A member from Utah was visiting a wealthy member friend in Arizona. Quizzing one another, the member from Utah asked what state he thought Adam and Eve were from? Thinking his friend would say Missouri (for that is what the teachings of the early Brethren say), he was surprised by this answer, "There is no doubt they were from Utah."

"Utah?"

Smiling, the Arizona friend quipped, "Yes, they had nothing to wear, nothing to eat but an apple, and still thought they lived in Paradise!"

Showing her son, age 7, a photo of his great-grandparents, Sister Ford explained they had lived a long time ago.

"I think I heard about them," he replied, "Were their names Adam and Eve?"

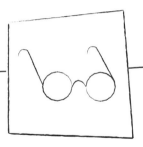

AGING

Aging is a natural process of mortality. The following are the lighter side of aging for some Latter-day Saints:

At their grandmother's birthday party, two grandchildren asked her how old she was.

"I'm 68," replied Sister Smith.

The oldest grandchild kindly said, "You sure don't look it."

The youngest grandchild leaned toward his sister and whispered, "But parts of her do."

An older Bishop once remarked, "If you want to stay young, associate with the youth in the ward. If you want to feel your age, try to keep up with them!"

A father in a ward explained, "The best years of my life are when the kids are old enough to mow the lawn, but too young to drive the family car."

Many Saints know that they have reached the "Age of Metals" when—
Their teeth are partially gold,
Their hair has turned to silver,
And, they have lead in their pants.

An older High Councilman began his talk about the resurrection with this wry statement, "Death is a congenital birth defect."

In another ward, this same High Councilman began this same talk with this statement, "Life is a terminal disease."

With a twinkle in her eye, an older Relief Society member quipped, "I've reached the age where my happy hour is a nap."

On another occasion, this same Relief Society member stated, "I'm at the age where 'getting it together' means bifocals."

Speaking to the young women in her ward, an 80-year-old sister said, "You know when you're old—when you reach down to get the wrinkles out of your nylons, and you realize you aren't wearing any."

While still speaking to the young woman, this same sister said she had finally learned this great truth, "Though not desirable, wrinkles don't hurt!"

Using a cane, 79-year-old Brother said to his returned missionary grandson, "The trouble with being old is—it's a 24-hour a day job."

The oldest High Priest in the ward slowly said to his Bishop, "I'll turn 100 years old tomorrow, and I want you to know that I don't have an enemy in the world."

"That's wonderful," the Bishop replied.

"Yes sir," said the High Priest, "I've outlived every one of them."

One High Priest asked his fellow High Priest how he was doing. The one answered, "I'm in good shape—for the shape I'm in."

A High Priest teased his fellow High Priest about his shape. The one replied, "I'm in shape—round is a shape!"

A granddaughter, age 6, asked her grandfather if he'd go down the pool slide one more time. He declined, explaining he was tired and "very out of shape."

"Oh, no, Grandpa," was her innocent response. "You have lots of shapes."

A sister in a ward asked another sister: "How are you feeling today?"

She responded, "I think I'm fine, but I'm not soliciting a second opinion."

Speaking about finances with her granddaughter, an older sister stated, "In spite of the cost of living—it's still popular."

Encouraging the High Priests to exercise regularly, the High Priest Group Leader quipped, "Pushing sixty is not exercise enough."

Being teased about his receding hair, the High Priest Group Leader replied, "I'm not going bald; I'm gaining face."

Spotting his grandfather sitting in a chair, a young grandson reached up and gently patted the man's balding head.

"Grandpa, your hair is growing!" he excitedly reported. "It's almost up to the top of your head."

A grandfather had a partial denture, which his 3-year-old granddaughter had seen him remove several times. One day she was sitting on her grandfather's lap. After touching his receding hairline, she innocently asked, "Do you take your hair off?"

Speaking to her teenage granddaughters, a sister reminded them, "At twenty, we don't care what the world thinks of us. At thirty, we don't worry about what it thinks of us. At sixty, we finally discover it wasn't even thinking of us."

On another occasion, this same sister told her teenage granddaughters, "We are only young once, but we can be immature indefinitely."

She added, "Growing old is mandatory; growing up is optional."

While watching her grandmother carefully applying makeup, a 3-year-old granddaughter said, "I don't need that stuff, Grandma. I'm too new!"

Having overheard my husband and I discuss the ailments of people we knew, one of our younger children pointed out an older woman in the grocery store who was walking by with some effort. Our child noticed her legs and said, "Mommy, that lady has 'very close veins.'"

—Else Lunden

A 73-year-old brother told his neighbor, "Nothing is more depressing than to feel bad in the morning without having had any fun the night before."

On another occasion, this same brother told his neighbor, "You're getting old when you get the same sensation from a rocking chair that you once got from a roller coaster."

A Bishop went to visit an older brother in the ward who hadn't been to Church for several years. After a cordial conversation, the Bishop said, "You know, Bob, you're not getting any younger. Don't you think it's time you started to thinking of the here-after?"

"Oh, I do," the man replied. "Several times a day I go to my closet and say, 'Now, what is it I'm here after?'"

Talking to his grandson, Brother Jones said, "The good thing about growing old is that you can whistle while you brush your teeth."

A photographer was asked to take a photo of a brother on his 98th birthday.

Observing that the elderly man was in such good health, the photographer commented, "You are a very young acting 98-year-old; perhaps I'll have the opportunity of taking your photo when you're 100?"

"I don't know why not," replied this Brother, "you look healthy enough too me."

A middle-aged brother returned from his missionary reunion and told to his family that he was not attending any future reunions. He said, "My old companions have gotten so overweight and bald that they scarcely recognize me."

An older brother noticed that his married, middle-age grandson was gaining weight. He gently teased, "You know you've reached middle-age when your wife tells you to pull in your stomach, and you already have."

Some cereal boxes contain a toy inside. Brother Todd watched his young grandson excitedly open such a box and said, "Middle age is when you choose your cereal for the fiber, not for the toy."

When a granddaughter asked what year her grandmother was born, Sister Ray told her, '36.
It really aged Sister Ray when the girl responded, "Was that 1836 or 1936?"

While recovering from surgery, a 75-year-old woman told her 25-year-old granddaughter, "Time may be a great healer, but it's a lousy beautician."
Later, a grandson was complimenting this grandmother about her wisdom.
She wryly answered, "Wisdom comes with age, but sometimes age comes alone."

I ran across an older High Priest friend and asked, "Paul, how are you doing?"

With a smile on his face, he wryly answered, "I'm mildewing."

When a young couple moved into a ward, they asked their Bishop the age of the ward.

He quipped, "The range is from newly wed to nearly dead!"

ATTITUDE

Many factors affect our attitude in life. The goal of every member of the Church is to have a happy and positive attitude, no matter what challenges and trials he or she encounters in life. The following are the lighter side of attitude.

While at an Elder's Quorum party, a couple was talking to another couple about the challenge of taking their young children on a trip. One Elder quipped, "A well-adjusted man is one who can enjoy the scenery—even with the kids in the back seat of the car."

A sister in a ward was always gossiping and murmuring about the members of her ward. When she spoke, everyone listened because it was always so juicy and alarming.

One day, the Relief Society President visited this sister at her home and challenged her to go two weeks without murmuring, gossiping or finding fault with anyone. This sister was a little embarrassed by the request, but answered, "Well, if you want me to, I'll try it."

After two weeks, the Relief Society President visited this sister at her home and asked, "How did you do with your challenge?"

"It wasn't easy, but I did it." Looking directly at the Relief Society President, she declared, "And I want you to know that it was the dullest two weeks of my life!"

‥‿

A Bishop visited an overweight man who had been home from his mission for four years and was still single. During their conversation, the Bishop asked the young man how his life was going.

"Terrible, Bishop," the man said. "I'm overweight and none of the young women will even give me a chance to date. I really want to lose weight, but I can't get motivated about exercising. I want to get married, but the most attractive girls pay no attention to me."

To his surprise, the Bishop said, "I can help get you in shape and introduce you to some young women who are interested in marriage, if you'll agree to follow a very simple plan. Tomorrow morning, be ready to exercise and I'll provide the incentive."

The man agreed, feeling excited about losing weight and finding a beautiful, young lady to possibly marry. The next morning at 7:00 a.m. this young man was up, dressed in his sweatsuit and ready for exercise.

There was a knock on his door and when he opened it he saw one of the most beautiful, slender girls from the ward, also dressed in a sweatsuit. She said, "The Bishop told me to tell you that we should exercise together with the understanding that if you catch me, I'll marry you." She then started running down the street.

After hearing this challenge, the young man ran out the front door after this young woman. However, she was quick and was some distance in front of him. After 20 minutes of running, the young man was panting and knew that he couldn't catch the woman. She stopped down the street and yelled that she would be back the next morning, and he could try to catch her again.

Sure enough, she was there the next morning. Day after day this continued. After several weeks of running, the young man was losing weight, gaining more speed, and he felt more confident of catching this attractive young woman.

The Bishop finally checked on the man and asked how things were going. "Great!, he said. "It won't be long before I catch the young woman you sent."

The Bishop observed the young man's shape was improving, but that he still needed to lose weight.

The next morning when the doorbell rang, the young man was eager to begin the chase. When he opened the door, instead of seeing the attractive young woman, he was surprised to see an unattractive, overweight young lady. She said, "The Bishop told me that you wanted to run this morning, and if I could catch you during the run, you would marry me!"

Highly motivated by this statement, the man discovered that he could run faster than he had previously thought possible.

BIBLE STORIES
(THE LIGHTER SIDE)

With some background information given first, the following stories are about events, people, and places in the Bible.

DAVID

When he was younger, David was highly favored of the Lord. He was chosen by the Lord to become the king of Israel.

When David was a young man, the armies of Israel and the Philistines engaged in war. David went against the giant Goliath in the name of the Lord, and David killed Goliath with a sling and a stone. The following is the lighter side of that story, as written by a child:

"David fought with the Finkelsteins, a race of people who lived in Biblical times."

The following questions and answers about David and Goliath have been told for years:

24

Question: Who was the greatest babysitter mentioned in the Bible?
Answer: David—he rocked Goliath to sleep.

Question: Why was Goliath so surprised when David hit him with a stone from a slingshot?
Answer: The thought had never before entered his mind.

After the story of David and Goliath was told in a Primary class, Ryan was asked by Sister Stephens, "What would you do if you were in David's place today?"
He responded seriously, "I'd call 911."

HOLY LAND

While visiting the Holy Land, a guide explained to an LDS travel group how the country extended from the land of Dan even to Beersheba.
Sister Larson said innocently to the lecturer, "I didn't realize Dan and Beersheba were actual places. I always thought they were a man and wife, like Sodom and Gomorrah."

A Primary teacher was teaching her class about the Promised Land. She asked, "What do you think a land flowing with milk and honey would look like?"
A boy responded, "Sticky."

A Sunday school teacher asked, "Sarah, what do we know about the Dead Sea?"

Knowing nothing about it, Sarah answered, "Dead? I didn't even know it was ill."

LOT'S WIFE

Lot was a nephew of the Prophet Abraham. He traveled with Abraham to Canaan. While living in Sodom, Lot entertained holy men. Lot, his wife, and their two daughters were sent out of Sodom because the Lord was going to destroy it and the city of Gomorrah. The holy men said to Lot: "Escape for thy life; look not behind thee, neither stay thou in all the plain; escape to the mountain, lest thou be consumed." (Gen. 19:15-17)

As brimstone and fire rained from heaven upon Sodom and Gomorrah, Lot's "wife looked back from behind him, and she became a pillar of salt." (Gen.19:24-26; See also Luke 17:32-33)

A primary teacher described how Lot's wife looked back at Sodom and was turned into a pillar of salt.

Suddenly Jimmy interrupted, "My mother looked back once while she was driving the car, and she turned into a telephone pole!"

Question: What were Lot's last words to his wife?
Answer: "Honey, are the girls still following us?"

MOSES

Latter-day revelation concerning Moses confirms the biblical account of his his divine calling as a prophet of God.

The following questions and answers have been told about Moses for years:

Question: Who was the greatest female financier in the Bible?
Answer: Pharoah's daughter—she went down to the bank of the Nile and drew out a little prophet.

An inactive member of the Church asked her 9-year-old son: "What did you learn in Primary today?"

"We learned how Moses led the Israeli amphibious battalion into the Red Sea against a large Egyptian Army, and by superior military strategy completely destroy the Pharoah's Air Force, Navy, and Marines in one afternoon."

"Are you sure that's what the teacher said?"

"Well, not exactly Mom, but you would never believe it the way the teacher told it."

Question: Which servant of God was the most active law breaker in the Bible?
Answer: Moses—he broke all of the commandments at one time.

Question: Where is medicine first mentioned in the
        Bible?
Answer: When God gave Moses two tablets.

Question: Who was known as a Mathematician in
        the Bible?
Answer: Moses—he wrote the book of Numbers.

NOAH

Noah was a preacher of righteousness who
happened to build a really big boat in the process.
The following jokes are the lighter side of Noah and
the flood.

After reading about Noah, a younger grandson
surprised his grandmother by saying he knew the
name of Noah's wife.

"I don't think the Bible tell us what her name
was," she said.

"Oh yes it does," he insisted.

"It says that Noah found Grace in the eyes of the
Lord." (See Gen. 6:8)

Another child confidently told his Primary class,
"Noah's wife was called Joan of Ark."

When explaining about the animals entering the ark, a child wrote, "Noah built an ark, which the animals came to in pears."

Question: Who was the greatest financier in the Bible?
Answer: Noah—he was floating his stock while everyone else was in liquidation.

Question: The top story of the ark had windows to let light in, but how did Noah get light to the bottom two stories?
Answer: He used floodlights.

Question: What was Noah's greatest worry on the ark?
Answer: Protecting the pair of mosquitoes.

Question: Where did Noah keep the bees?
Answer: In the Ark-hives.

After having a family home evening lesson on Noah and the ark, a young boy turned to his grandpa and asked, "Were you on Noah's ark?"
    "No," the grandpa said with a laugh.
    The boy replied, "Then why didn't you drown?"

BISHOP

One of the ordained offices in the Aaronic Priesthood is that of Bishop. He is the president of the Aaronic Priesthood in his ward and is also the president of the priests' quorum.

A Bishop is also the presiding high priest in his ward, and he presides over all ward affairs and members.

While speaking with his Stake President, a Bishop admitted, "I have a hard time remembering the last names of certain people when they are introduced."

"So do I," the Stake President replied. "But I found a way to get around the awkwardness of asking them to repeat their name later. I just ask, 'Do you spell your last name with an 'E' or with an 'I'"?

The Bishop thought that sounded like a good idea and would give it a try.

Several weeks later the Stake President was visiting with the Bishop and asked him, "How has the new way for learning the names of certain people gone for you?"

"It worked well several times," replied the Bishop, "but then one family who moved in the ward, I asked them if they spelled their last name with an 'E' or and 'I' and they got quite upset. I don't know if they will come back to Church or not."

"What was their last name?"

"Hill."

A Bishop had called several individuals to serve as a teacher in the ward but no one would accept the call. Finally, a sister in the ward accepted it.

In Sacrament Meeting, the Bishop stood at the pulpit and tried to make those members who had not accepted the call to feel guilty, and to compliment the sister who did accept it. However, it didn't go over as intended.

The Bishop sternly said, "Brothers and sisters, we have called several individuals to an important teaching position and no one accepted it." After a pause, he continued, "After scraping the bottom of the barrel—we finally came up with Sister Erickson."

—Clair Leavitt

A young child was putting up a fuss in Sacrament Meeting. Having no success at calming his boy, the father picked up the lad and started for the side door. As they neared the door, the child yelled out, "Save me, Bishop!"

A new Bishop received a phone call from an inactive sister in his ward who expressed a desire to get her life in order and repent of her sins.

The Bishop arranged for an appointment with her for the following week. Then he visited the previous Bishop and said to him, "Sister Jones wants to get her life in order. I have never dealt with a moral issue of this magnitude before, and I desperately need you to be there at the meeting."

The released Bishop said, "Hold on there. I've been released. Those meetings are confidential, and I shouldn't be there."

Every day during that week, the new Bishop visited the released Bishop with the same plea. The day before the meeting with the sister, the new Bishop said in desperation to the released Bishop, "Please just sit in the clerk's office. I'll leave the door slightly open, and you can critique me afterward."

Exasperated, the released Bishop finally agreed to sit in the clerk's office, but firmly stated, "Never again."

A few minutes before the sister arrived at the office, the released Bishop was escorted into the clerk's office. Sister Jones then arrived and gave the new Bishop a detailed explanation about her life, including some real eyebrow raisers!

After Sister Jones left, the new Bishop asked the old Bishop to critique him. The released Bishop said, "Well, you did a pretty good job. However, let me give you a few pointers. At times you just need to say, 'Hmm' or 'Uh huh,' instead of loudly saying each time, 'You did that?'"

On the Sunday before New Year's Day, a new Bishop told the congregation that when he had been made Bishop, he had set a goal of visiting every family in the ward before the year ended.

Apologizing that he had not met this goal, he asked anyone to raise their hand if they had been missed and really needed a visit before the end of the year.

Only one person raised her hand—the Bishop's wife.

A Bishop visited his next door neighbor, an inactive member of his ward. After a cordial conversation, the Bishop forthrightly asked, "John, what do you have against coming to Church?"

John wryly answered, "The first time I went to Church, they threw me in the water. The second time, they tied me to a woman I have had to support ever since."

With a smile on his face, the Bishop responded, "And the next time, they will probably throw dirt on you afterward."

A wife went into her husband's bedroom and said, "Come on now, it's time to get up. It's time to go to Church."

The husband pulled the covers over his head and groaned, "I don't want to go. I'm staying in bed."

His wife replied, "You really ought to go. It's important."

The husband stuck his head out from under the covers and said, "Give me one good reason for going to Church today."

His wife replied, "Because you're the Bishop!"

Several Bishops were flying to attend General Conference in Salt Lake City when one of the plane's engines quit. A pretty stewardess hurried about, assuring the passengers that everything would be okay.

One of the Bishops felt the stewardess needed a little assurance herself. He told her, "Nothing will happen to this plane, for there are eight LDS Bishops aboard."

The stewardess forced a smile and said she would relay the comforting news to the pilot.

After visiting with the pilot, she hurried back to the Bishop and replied, "I told the pilot there were eight LDS Bishop's aboard, but he said, 'No offense intended, but I'd rather have four good engines.'"

The chapel was filled to capacity for Sacrament Meeting. Shortly after the meeting started, the Bishop noticed that the Stake Presidency had made a surprise visit and were standing near the chapel's back door.

Since there were no empty seats on the stand, the Bishop leaned forward and softly said to one of the Deacons on the front row, "Robert, please go get me three chairs."

Because the Bishop spoke so softly, Robert only partially heard him. So he replied, "What?"

Not wanting the entire congregation to hear, the Bishop whispered back, "Get me three chairs."

Still not properly hearing the Bishop, Robert again asked, "What?"

Getting a little impatient, the Bishop said, "Get me three chairs, now."

Robert looked at the Bishop and said, "Now?"

The Bishop replied, "Now."

Being obedient, Robert shrugged his shoulders, jumped to his feet, and yelled, "Rah, Rah, Rah, Bishop!"

A Bishop, a Stake President and an IRS agent died the same day. When they arrived at the pearly gates, Saint Peter greeted them.

After listening to them explain what they had each done in life, Peter turned to the IRS agent and said, "We've been waiting for you. Please come in."

He then turned to the Bishop and Stake President and said, "I'll need more information about you before you can come in."

Surprised, they each asked why an IRS agent would be able to go right in and they would have to wait.

St. Peter answered, "My records show that the IRS agent scared the Devil out of more people than you two put together."

BUDGET
(MONEY)

No matter what a person earns financially, he or she must learn to budget their money. There are many challenges and rewards of budgeting one's income. The following are the lighter side of budgeting money for some members of the Church.

During a Relief Society lesson on budgeting money, Sister Jones wittingly made this statement, "Many times Mama's yearning capacity is many times greater than Papa's earning capacity!"

Then toward the end of her remarks, she added, "I almost have a Siamese twin relationship with my husband—we're joined together at the wallet."

A Bishopric counselor who usually had a cheery disposition was not very jovial after a bishopric meeting. The Bishop asked the counselor if anything was troubling him.

"Well, lately my wife has been buying items on the lay-awake-plan," he said.

"You mean the lay-away plan?" asked the Bishop.

"No, I meant what I said. My wife buys things we can't afford, then I lay awake at night wondering how we're going to pay for them."

Several young couples in a college ward were having a combined family home evening lesson on finances. To emphasize the importance of budgeting, Brother Ward wittingly said, "It's nice to have the highest standard of living in the world—too bad we can't afford it."

Later he commented, "Every time a family gets a little bit ahead financially—it usually discovers something it hadn't needed previously."

After co-signing with his son to purchase his first car, Brother Williams quipped to his son, "If you think nobody cares if you're alive, trying missing a couple of these car payments."

Speaking to the Relief Society members about budgeting money for charitable contributions, the Bishop quoted this saying:

"Render under Caesar that which is Caesar's

"And unto God that which is God's

"But did you know that which you render unto God—is tax deductible?"

Speaking with his recently married son about family finances, Brother Fines lamented, "You'll soon learn that a father is a man who has pictures in his wallet where his money used to be."

Sister Tyler told her newly married daughter about the time when she was a newlywed. "The only way your father and I ever balanced our budget was the ad hoc approach," she said. "If we wanted to buy something, we had to hock something else."

During an Elder's Quorum meeting on budgeting, Brother Allen quipped, "Money won't buy happiness, but it's a lot easier to cope with depression in a Cadillac than in an old Volkswagen."

During Sacrament Meeting, a High Councilman explained that he had experienced his share of financial struggles in life. He said, "While attending graduate school, money was a scarce commodity with me and my wife. One evening when my wife came home from work, she was wearing a new, fancy dress. Cautiously she approached me and said, 'Now, honey, don't get mad, just tell me how you like it.'

"I had to admit that it looked real nice. But I told myself I had to be firm, so I said, 'Dear, why did you buy that dress? You know that we can't afford it.'

"At this comment, my wife started to cry. She said, 'I don't know why I bought it—the Devil must have tempted me.'

"I then said to her, 'You've heard it said that when the Devil tempts you, you should say to him, "Get thee behind me, Satan."'

"'I did,' she sobbed.

"'What did he say?' I asked.

"He said, 'Boy, that dress sure looks great from the back!'"

Speaking to family members about budgeting money for unexpected medical bills, Brother Smith quipped, "When you get your hospital bill—you understand why surgeons wear masks in the operating room."

While teaching a History class at a local high school, Sister Kitter asked, "Now that we have completed our study of the Constitution of the United States, who can tell me how the principle of checks and balances works in American society?"

One of the students raised his hand and said, "At home, Mom writes the checks and Dad struggles to keep them in balance."

CHILDREN
(THE LIGHTER SIDE)

Every person who is born on this earth is a child of God. Each has a unique personality. Each child views things in life with different levels of understanding. Here is the lighter side of what some children have said.

It was time to go to Church, so a mother told her 3-year-old daughter to put her shoes on. Later, the mother noticed that her daughter's shoes were on wrong and she explained, "Your shoes are on the wrong feet."

This daughter answered sincerely, "But Mom, it's the only feet I have."

Upon returning home from Church, a mother told her young daughter to change out of her good clothes. Puzzled, she pointed at her everyday clothes and asked, "Are these my naughty ones?"

One evening, a five-year-old nephew was riding home with his aunt and uncle. Suddenly in the sky, each saw a falling star.

This lad was fascinated with this sighting, and he wanted to know where it might land. The aunt explained that it might fall in a field or someone's backyard. Then she said, "It might even fall in the ocean."

At this comment, he smiled and clapped his hands. He said, "Now I know how starfish are made!"

Right before a daughter started first grade, she heard different family members talk about how quickly the years pass. One family member said to this young girl that in no time she would be grown and have a family of her own.

After getting off the bus after her first day of school, this daughter ran up to the house. Inside, she shouted, "I'm home, Mom."

Then excitedly she said to her mother, "It won't be long now before you're a grandma!"

While driving along one evening, a grandma and grandpa were admiring a beautiful half-moon.

In the back seat of the car, their 5-year-old granddaughter stared intently at the moon for a long time. "Grandma," she finally said, "the other half of that moon needs a new light bulb."

On a trip to Niagara Falls, this mother was standing with both arms around her 3-year-old son, taking in the inspiring sight. After having seen enough, this lad asked, "When is this thing going to fill up?"

A daughter was very young when her parents took her to visit Niagara Falls one afternoon. When this family returned to this scenic sight early the next morning, this daughter questioned, "Mom, did they let it run all night long?"

A young son wanted a brother. One day, while driving in the car, this mother read to this boy a billboard promoting a motel's special rate. "Kids are free," the advertisement read.

This young lad's face suddenly brightened. "Oh, Mom," he excitedly said, "can we stop and get one?"

A granddaughter intently looked at her grandmother's hands, and asked, "Why do you have so many wrinkles?"

"I guess I'm just getting old," this grandmother answered.

With that comment, this granddaughter looked at her hands and declared, "Not me—I'm almost brand-new!"

One evening when a nephew was visiting his aunt and uncle, they looked at the bright, white moon for a few minutes. Later, when the TV was playing, the weather man said that it was going to be a 'blue moon.' To this statement, this nephew said to his aunt and uncle, "I guess that he doesn't know his colors very well."

After a full day of swimming and playing in the sun, two young, weary daughters were getting ready for bed.

One said, "Look, Mom,' the 3-year-old said excitedly, after looking at her reddened skin in the mirror, "I got a fun burn."

While getting ready for bed, a 4-year-old said to her mother, "It is funny—every time I put my pajamas on, it gets dark outside."

A son, age 2, was listening intently to his dad explain that on his way to work that morning, he had stopped his car to let a mother bear and her two little cub walk across the road.

"Wow!" he exclaimed, "Did you see Goldilocks, too?"

During a recent visit, a grandmother told her energetic 4-year-old granddaughter to find something peaceful to do for an afternoon "quiet time."

After a few minutes the grandmother finished reading the newspaper, and the granddaughter eagerly broke the silence with, "Can we have loud time now?"

As a mother and father were looking at new cars, this mother said to her husband, "It sure would be great to get a mini-van."

Upon hearing that, their 2-year-old son asked, "Can we get a Mickey-van, too?"

A six-year-old son asked permission to open his medicine by himself. After he had struggled turning and twisting the cap awhile, his mother explained that the bottle had a childproof cap.

Exasperated, this boy looked at his mother and queried, "How does the cap know I'm a child?"

It was well-known among the grandchildren that their grandmother gave them money for birthdays. This grandmother had to chuckle when one of the younger ones asked, "Do we get raises as we get older?"

A 3-year-old boy was sitting on his great-grandmother's lap looking through a catalog in search of new pajamas.

When this great-grandmother recommended he get a pair with feet, he responded, "I already have feet!"

After having played in the tub for awhile, a granddaughter, age 4, wiggled her wrinkled fingers and laughed, "I have Granny hands!"

On a trip to town, a young grandson asked his grandmother if they could stop for ice cream with strawberries and whipped cream on top.

"Do you mean a sundae?" the grandmother asked.

He replied, "No, Grandma—I mean today!"

Instead of saying "good-bye," a grandson's doctor told him, "Hasta la vista."

The 4-year-old boy's Spanish wasn't very good when he replied back, "Happy Easter to you, too!"

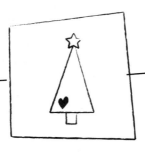

CHRISTMASTIME

Santa Claus is the American Dutch version of the name of the Saint Nicholas, a noted Catholic bishop, who lived in the second or third century. This bishop was a very generous old gentleman, so much so that he was called the patron-saint of children and youth.

In the early centuries, his memory was perpetuated on the 6th day of December by a member of the family dressing in the costume of a bishop and appearing among the children laden with gifts for the good children and mild punishment for the naughty ones.

When the custom was brought over to America by the early Dutch settlers in New York, it had already become fixed to the 25th day of December.

Many in the world celebrate December 25th as the traditional day our Lord's mortal birth. Though there are various opinions by scholars, both in and out of the Church, concerning the day our Lord was born in mortality, it is believed He was actually born on April 6th. (See D&C 20:1)

The Latter-day Saints join in the wholesome portions of the Christmas celebration. Christmas, then, becomes an ideal opportunity to renew their search for the true Spirit of Christ and to center their attention again on the true doctrine of his birth, as told in the New Testament by Luke and Matthew.

The following are the lighter side of Christmastime:

At a Christmas High Priest social, a High Priest Group Leader told the audience, "This time of year reminds me of the four stages of life: First, you believe in Santa Claus. Second, you don't believe in Santa Claus. Third, you are Santa Claus. And, fourth, you look like Santa Claus!"

One Christmas, our 3-year-old surveyed all the presents Santa had brought her and happily beamed, "I didn't know I was this good!"

—Darlene Bindle

A department store Santa had a long line of children waiting to talk to him. Some of the children were more anxious than others to sit on Santa's knee and tell what they wanted for Christmas.

Finally, one little girl hurried and sat on this Santa's knee. "Ho, ho, ho," said Santa. "What do you want most of all?"

"I want to know where the bathroom is!" she replied.

While taking her three grandchildren Christmas shopping, Sister Erickson was told by her oldest granddaughter, age 10, to look at the sign over the toy section in the store.

It read: "If You See Something You Want, Tell Grandma!"

At a Relief Society Christmas social, Sister Wilkinson quoted the following poem:

Christmas is the magic time of year
    When the year runs out,
    The neighbors run in,
    The batteries run down,
    And the bills run up!

On a break, Brother Rose was telling his fellow co-workers what his wife told him about buying her a Christmas gift:

"My wife is the subtle type. This morning she told me I didn't need to shop early for her Christmas present because—'Diamonds are forever!'"

Brother Darrell Corbridge played Santa one Christmas. He helped put a little girl on his lap and said, "Ho, ho, ho, what do you want for Christmas this year?"

The little girl looked at him funny and said, "You need a breath mint!"

A MISSIONARY CHRISTMAS

'Twas the night before Christmas
         And all through the mission
Each elder was tracting,
         At least we were wishing.

Me in my old suit
         The elder's in his, too
Sat down by the mailbox
         For our checks to come through.

When out on the street
         There arose such a clatter
We all looked to see
         What was the matter.

Was the traveling elders
         Dressed in missionary array
Who came to tract
         On this white Christmas day.

My heart skipped a beat
         And my mind had a thought
Tracting on Christmas
         Wasn't so hot!

When Sister Hyde opened her Christmas present from her husband, she happily said, "Thanks so much. This is just what I need to exchange for what I really want."

Before giving a lesson on the birth of Jesus at Christmastime, a Primary teacher asked, "Does anyone know the name of Jesus' mother?"

A young girl raised her hand and said, "Mary."

"That is correct," said the teacher.

The teacher then asked, "Does anyone know the name of Jesus' step-father?"

After thinking about it, a young boy said, "His name is Virg."

Surprised by the answer, the teacher asked, "How did you come up with that name?"

"Virg and Mary."

At a family Christmas party, Brother Campbell, who was a successful salesman, said, "I can relate to the Christmas story in some ways. For instance, when Joseph and Mary went to Bethlehem, they had to stay in a stable, because there was not room in the inn."

Then he quipped, "I've had travel agents like that myself."

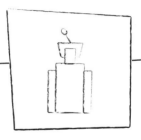

CHURCH LEADERS

"We believe in the same organization that existed in the Primitive Church, namely, apostles, prophets, pastors, teachers, evangelists, and so forth." (Sixth Article of Faith)

For administrative purposes, the Church is divided into stakes and missions. Each stake is composed of wards and branches. Various officers are called to serve in the wards and branches. Without listing all of the callings, the following stories share the lighter side of a few of them.

STAKE PRESIDENT

At a Stake Priesthood meeting, a Stake President gave the following advice, "Do you know why a little puppy has so many friends? It's because he has learned to wag his tail, not his tongue!"

At the conclusion of his remarks, he recited this humorous poem:

"Be careful of the words you say,
"Make them soft and sweet.
"For you never know from day to day,
"The ones you'll have to eat!"

At a ward conference, a Stake President went to the Primary to give a short talk to the children.

As he spoke to this large group of children, teachers, and leaders of the Primary, he asked if there was anyone who could tell him something about the Apostle Peter. A little girl raised her hand and waved it excitedly.

Encouraged to see someone so enthusiastic, the Stake President said, "Come up here, sweetheart. I'm glad to know that your mother and father have taught you lessons from the New Testament."

After the girl came and stood by him, this leader said, "Will you please tell all the other boys and girls what you know about the Apostle Peter?"

The little girl stepped up to the microphone, and clearly said, "Peter, Peter, pumpkin eater, had a wife and couldn't keep her. So, he . . . ."

Church headquarters uses a computer to keep track of how long Stake Presidents have served.

In accordance, my former Stake President, Vincent Erickson, made this witty observation: "Stake Presidents are called by inspiration, but are released by computer!"

When President Wallis was released, he said to the congregation, "I've just gone from 'Who's Who,' to 'Who's He?'"

HIGH COUNCIL MEMBER

A 16-year-old young man brought a non-member friend to Sacrament Meeting. The Bishop announced that the first speaker would be Brother Johnson, a member of the ward who had been called to serve as a high council member.

The non-member asked his member friend, "What does that mean?"

The member replied, "Oh, it means Brother Johnson is going to give a talk today."

Brother Johnson stood at the pulpit, looked at the congregation and opened his Bible.

"What does that mean?" asked the non-member.

"That means he is going to preach from the Bible." the young man responded.

Then, Brother Johnson took off his wrist watch and placed it on the pulpit. "What does that mean?" asked the non-member friend.

"It doesn't mean a thing!" the young man said.

Brother David Suisse spoke in the ward I attend. He said, "Of all the wards in the stake, I keep getting assigned to this ward more than others. It must be because you have a higher tolerance for pain."

Later in his talk, he said that when one of his sons was young, this boy had done something to make him become quite angry. While getting in his son's face, he was really lecturing this boy. When Brother Suisse was through, the son turned to his mother and said, "Dad sure has bad breath!"

Brother Alton told the ward members the advice the Stake President had given the high council members concerning their speaking assignments: "Remember, speakers should finish before the congregation does!"

In his Sacrament meeting talk, Brother Ritter said, "When I was reading the scriptures the other day, the word of the Lord came to me loud and clear. So, if you want to know what the Lord said to me, please open to D&C 112:5."

After several members turned to the passage, they began to snicker. Brother Ritter then read to the congregation, ". . . let not the inhabitants of the earth slumber, because of thy speech."

After arriving home from speaking in a ward, Sister Todd asked her husband, "How was your talk?"

This high council member answered, "It went so well that the whole congregation was open-mouthed."

"Really?" asked Sister Todd.

"Yes. They all yawned at once."

Brother Tidbits said in Sacrament Meeting that some members call high council members, "Dry council members." Admitting that some speakers are better than others, he said he was going to quote a poem about dry, high council speakers in meetings:

"If this world were to be flooded,
"To this meeting I would fly.
"For this world could be flooded,
"And this meeting would still be dry."

BRANCH PRESIDENT

A member from Salt Lake City was visiting a friend in a small branch in Kentucky. Sister Rowland remarked, "Karen, you certainly have a small congregation."

"Yes," she agreed, "It is so small that at times when the Branch President says, 'Dearly beloved,' I feel like I've received a proposal."

Continuing, Karen said to her friend, "If this Branch gets any smaller, it will be called a Twig!"

HIGH PRIEST

While speaking at a High Priest social, the High Priest Group leader told the brethren, "A fellow co-worker told me that someone had recently died in his High Priest classroom. The paramedics carried out three brethren before they found the right one!"

A ward Bishop was holding a leadership meeting. A baby in the nearby nursery was crying and making it difficult for the Bishop to conduct the meeting. He excused himself and left the room.

After a couple of minutes, this Bishop returned and continued the meeting. Not a sound was heard from the baby.

At the end of the meeting, a ward member asked him how he got the baby to be quiet. "Easy," the Bishop jokingly said, "I ordained him a High Priest and he went right to sleep."

ELDERS QUORUM PRESIDENT

Two sisters of a ward were discussing what they should wear to the Elder's Quorum social. The one said, "We're supposed to wear something to match our husband's hair, so I am going to wear something brown."

Turning to the Elder's Quorum President's wife, she asked, "What are you going to wear?"

"Goodness," gasped the other, "If I have to wear something to match my husband's hair—I don't think I better go!"

After having moved three families into the ward within a week with no help whatsoever from one of his counselors, President Jones felt the need to gently tease the counselor.

He told him, "Brother Holland, did you know that some people are like blisters—they don't show up until the work is done!"

PRIEST ADVISOR

A Priest Advisor was speaking to the quorum about countries with few members of the Church and how members can contribute funds to help them. He said, "In parts of Africa, there are hundreds of cities where they have no Church buildings. Now what should we all strive to save our money for?"

"To go to Africa," said one of the young men.

One Sunday, a Priest Advisor asked his priests this question: "Who can tell me who was most upset when the Prodigal Son returned home after wasting his father's money on riotous living?"

The class was quiet. Then, one boy quipped, "The fatted calf."

PRIMARY PRESIDENT

A Primary President was explaining to the children the story of Elijah the Prophet and the false prophets of Baal. She explained how Elijah built the altar, put wood upon it, cut the steer in pieces and laid it upon the altar.

Then she told how Elijah commanded the people of God to fill four barrels of water and pour it over the altar three times.

"Now," said the Primary President, "can anyone tell my why the Prophet Elijah had the people pour water over the steer on the altar?"

A little girl in the back of the room raised her hand quickly. She then said enthusiastically, "To make the gravy!"

After taking a noisy boy from a Primary class into the hallway, the Primary President spent a few minutes explaining how he should be good and reverent in class.

Then she said, "If you keep being noisy, Steven, perhaps I will not see you in heaven."

"Why?" asked Steven innocently. "What have you been doing wrong?"

A young girl was about to say her part in a Primary program. When she stood in front of the group, her carefully rehearsed lines faded from her mind and she stood there unable to utter a single syllable.

Soon, the Primary President knelt besides this girl and quietly asked if she needed help. The young girl didn't say a word.

The President noticed this girl's mother had quickly moved from the back to the front row, so the President sat down.

This mother whispered to her daughter, "Remember what I taught you at home, 'I am the light of the world.'"

Instantly the girl's face relaxed, a smile appeared and with confidence she began, "My mother is the light of the world."

RELIEF SOCIETY PRESIDENT

During a Relief Society meeting, the sisters were discussing the challenges and rewards of raising children. The Relief Society President told of listening to two of her relatives talking about their younger children. The one had said, "Are you troubled by the fact that your children occasionally tell lies?"

The other replied, "Not nearly as much as when they tell the truth at inappropriate times."

"When my brother was young," said a Relief Society President, "he thought that Relief Society was my mother's relief from the children at home."

YOUNG WOMEN PRESIDENT

Last week in the Mia Maid class, the lesson was entitled: "The Rich Young Man," and the reading assignment was "One Thing Thou Lackest."

This week, the Young Women President asked if anyone in the class remembered what they had studied last week. One young lady wittingly repeated, "One Thing Thou Lackest—A Rich Young Man!"

A Young Women's President told the Beehive class how blessed each was for having such a choice mother. Sister Ladd then asked a young woman what she would like to do when she was as big as her mother.

Jenny answered teasingly, "Diet."

DEATH

When the scriptures speak of death, they ordinarily mean the natural or temporal death. This death consists in the separation of the spirit from the mortal body.

Thus, the physical body returns to the dust. It is just as important to die as to be born. And, without death there would be no mortality or eternal life.

On his death bed, Brother Henderson made his wife promise to buy a double cemetery plot and place two headstones side by side. On his, she was to write "Follow me." That way, every time she visited the grave, she would remember their love and remain faithful.

Brother Henderson died and his wife followed his wishes for his headstone.

However, on her headstone, she had this written: "To follow thee, I'm not content, until I know which way you went."

Sister Broderick was asked by her non-member neighbor to be with her when she visited a spiritualist. The neighbor wanted to try to get in contact with her deceased husband.

Though Sister Broderick was very hesitant about doing this, she finally agreed. During the visit, the spiritualist contacted the dead husband. The neighbor asked him, "Bob, are you happy now?"

"I'm very happy," was his reply.

"Are you happier than you were with me on earth?"

"Yes, far happier," came the voice.

"Tell me, Bob, what is it like in heaven?"

"Heaven?" asked Bob. "Who's in heaven?"

When it came to money, Brother Phelps was a real miser. He didn't trust banks, and he kept most of his money in paper bags under his bed.

After several years went by, Brother Phelps became old and feeble, and this affected his thinking. He said to his wife, "I don't believe I will be here much longer on this earth. When I die, I am going to take my money with me."

Being old herself, Sister Phelps' thinking was not as good as it was a few years earlier. So, she said to her husband, "How are you going to take your money with you?"

He replied, "I have taken the bags of money up in the attic. When I die, my spirit will grab them on my way up to heaven."

Two weeks later, Brother Phelps died at home. After the funeral was over and family and friends stopped visiting with Sister Phelps, she remembered what her husband had told her about the money.

Slowly she walked the stairs to the attic. After finding and opening the paper bags of money, Sister Phelps shook her head and said, "I told that old miser he should have put them in the basement."

With his wife and family near his bed, Brother Scott died. His spirit was soon in a spirit realm where he noticed there was a long line of men standing in a row. At the front of this line was a large sign which read: "Henpecked Husbands."

In another line, only one man stood. He nervously kept looking from side to side. In front of him was a large sign which read: "Non-henpecked Husbands."

St. Peter walked up to this man and kindly asked, "How come you're standing in this line?"

The man timidly answered, "Because my wife told me to!"

The story is told of an inactive member of the Church who was visited by an Elders Quorum President.

This inactive member was a good man who had good intentions. He welcomed the president to his home, listened to him, and then said, "I will; I intend to; I will do it."

He also said, "I will come to Church when I get straightened out."

The president continued to visit the man over the years, and the same story was told: "Well, when I get straightened out, I'll come to Church."

The president said, "I was eventually called on to speak at this man's funeral. Well, this time he was finally in Church, and just as he said, he was surely straightened out!"

Brother Sadler, his wife, and mother-in-law went on a vacation to Jerusalem. While they were there the mother-in-law passed away.

The undertaker told them, "You can have her shipped home for $5,000, or you can bury her here in the Holy Land for $300."

After discussing it with his wife, Brother Sadler said, "We will ship her home."

The undertaker asked, "Why would you spend $5,000 to ship your mother-in-law home, when it would be wonderful to be buried here and you would only spend $300."

Brother Sadler told the man: "If history serves me right, a man died and was buried here in Jerusalem, and three days later he rose from the dead. I just can't take a chance of that happening."

FAMILY

Among the Latter-day Saints, the family is the basic unit of the Church. True family organization is patriarchal in nature and is patterned after that organization which exists in heaven.

Emma, age six, asked, "Mommy, where did I come from?"

Thinking this was a good time to explain the facts of life, Sister Jack spent a few minutes talking about the birds and bees, and everything else a six-year-old should know.

Sister Jack then asked, "Now, Sweetheart, do you understand where you came from?"

"I guess," replied the young girl. "I just wondered, because Sarah said she came from Florida."

While giving advice to some of her married children, Sister Owens wittingly reminded them about their younger children: "What shouldn't be heard by little ears—shouldn't be said by big mouths!"

Brother Earl was the first male teacher in his ward Primary. After three weeks of teaching, a mother of one of Brother Earl's students asked her son, "How do you like your new teacher?"

"I don't know, Mom," he replied. "She keeps sending her husband."

Sister Wheeler and Sister Watkins were talking about family members. Sister Wheeler quipped, "The good news is when your son and daughter-in-law present you with a grandchild. The bad news is when it's for the entire summer."

After having a hectic day with her six children, Sister Petersen called her neighbor, the ward choir director, and said, "You know the song 'Love at Home'? The first line reads: 'There is beauty all around, when there's love at home.' Today, I believe those words should be changed to read: 'There is beauty all around, when there's no one home.'"

Sister Hathaway said to her neighbor, "Before I was married I had five ideas for raising children. Now I'm married, I have five children and no ideas."

For their Family Home Evening, the Riley family decided to look through a family photo album. When the children saw a handsome young man with dark, wavy hair, a teenage daughter asked, "Who is that?"

"Oh, that is your father," Sister Riley said.

"Really?" the teenage daughter asked. "Then who is the baldheaded man that lives with us?"

In Primary, a young girl drew a picture of the family of Jesus. When the teacher asked who the fourth person in the picture was, her answer was a classic: "This one is Jesus, here is Mary, and this is Joseph. The other one is a baby-sitter for when Mary and Joseph want to go out for the evening."

It was the first day of Primary for Mark and Todd. While waiting for opening exercises to begin, Mark asked, "What's new at your house?"

"I don't know," said Todd. "My parents spell everything."

Brother Thompson was talking with his new neighbor when he said, "Every summer I relearn the theory of relativity."

"How is that?" asked the neighbor.

"If you have a swimming pool, like we do, we're going to see a lot of relatives!"

Ryan was an only child who really wanted a brother to play with. Each evening, when his mother and father kneeled beside him, Ryan would pray for a little brother.

After many months of asking and nothing happening, Ryan finally stopped praying for a brother. During this time, Sister Pitcher was expecting a child, and she eventually delivered twin boys.

"Wow!" Ryan exclaimed when he heard the news. "It's a good thing I stopped praying when I did."

A grandmother, Sister Nettles, was visiting with some of her married granddaughters. They were speaking about the challenges of raising children. Sister Nettles told them, "Children are the salt of the earth. And as everyone knows, salt can give you high blood pressure."

Three new fathers-to-be were nervously pacing the waiting room floor when the nurse came in and said to one, "Congratulations, you're the father of twins."

"Wonderful," said the new father. "What a coincidence. I work for the Twin Pines Hotel."

A little later, the same nurse came in again and announced to another, "Congratulations, you're the father of triplets."

"What a coincidence," shouted the new father. "I work for Triple-A Auto."

At this moment, the third father-to-be fainted. When the nurse finally revived him, the nurse asked, "What's the matter?"

The man replied, "Quick, get me out of here. I work for 7-Up."

While teaching the Relief Society about the family, Sister Anthony quipped, "Youth is a time of changes. Between the ages of twelve and eighteen, a parent can age twenty years."

Soon expecting another child, Sister Powell said to her 4-year-old son, "Would you like to have a brother or a sister?"

Austin answered truthfully, "I'd rather have a pony."

Brother Hunter was visiting with various family members following the wedding of one of his sons. Giving advice to the new groom, Brother Hunter said, "Ryan, you are now the head of your new family."

Another married son, Robert quickly said, "Ryan, you will quickly learn that the wife is the neck that turns the head."

Later, Robert said to Ryan, "When my wife and I disagree on matters, I always say the last words— 'Yes, Dear.'"

One Sunday, Sister Ritter tended two of her younger grandchildren. She decided to tell them about the creation of Adam and Eve, and she read them Genesis 3:19: "In the sweat of thy face shalt thou eat bread, til thou return unto the ground; for out of it wast thou taken: for dust thou art, and unto dust shalt thou return."

Later that afternoon, Mindy looked under her grandmother's bed and noticed all the dust that had accumulated there. She hurried to her grandmother and asked, "Grandma, you have a lot of dust under your bed. Is someone coming or going?"

Chelsea, age 8, said to her mother, "It isn't fair. At night, you tell me I'm too little to stay up. Then in the morning, you say I'm too big to stay in bed!"

Years ago when Brother Carl Cordingley was young and unable to read, he sat by his mother in Sacrament Meeting. Pointing to the EXIT sign, Carl asked his mother, "What does that say?"

She answered, "Quiet."

With a play-on-words with his last name, he said, "A Cordingley, whenever I saw that sign, I was quiet."

My father, Edward Dana, has always had a witty sense of humor. After my sixth daughter was born, Dad said to me, "Bruce, I know the Lord has told us to multiply and replenish the earth. But you don't need to do it by yourself."

The George Lusk family spoke in my ward Sacrament Meeting. Brother Lusk said, "I'm the responsible person in my family. If anything goes wrong, I'm responsible."

Brother Hernandez asked his daughter, "How are your grades this semester in college?"
Rena replied, "They're underwater."
"What do you mean?"
"They are all below 'C' level."

An LDS child needed to bring an old shirt from home for a school project concerning drug prevention. His mother was busy and she hurriedly handed him an old T-shirt without examining it.

When he arrived home from school, she was embarrassed to see was written on the shirt.

On the front it read: "A Family is Forever." On the back it now read: "Be Smart, Don't Start."

Speaking with her children who were attending college, Sister Brody encouraged them to complete their education.

She told them, "Don't fail to get a good education while you're young. It will come in handy when you have to help with your children's homework."

Brother Jones was telling some of his fellow High Priests about his recent family vacation. He quipped, "We went on vacation for a change and a rest. The waiters got the change, and the travel agent got the rest."

Having a discussion with his wife about their family budget, Brother Hayes asked her, "Where does all the grocery money go that I give you?"

Sister Hayes said, "I'll give you one hint. Stand sideways and look in the mirror."

Three neighbor ladies were talking about their children going back to school in a week. Sister Speth quipped, "School days can be the happiest days of our lives—provided our children are old enough to go."

Family Home Evening may be the only family fight that begins and ends with prayer.

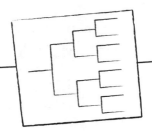

FAMILY RESEARCH

Before any vicarious ordinances of salvation can be performed for those who have died without a knowledge of the gospel of Jesus Christ, these people must be accurately and properly identified. Family history research has turned into a popular and important hobby for many Church members.

On Thanksgiving a grandson heard his sister and mother talking about their family's ancestors. Puzzled, he asked, "If we have 'ansisters,' do we have 'anbrothers,' too?"

—Marlene A.

While having lunch with two of his favorite boy cousins, a 4-year-old grandson stated to his grandparents, "Cousins are just like brothers—except they live in a different house."

After dating a young man three times, Sister Ritter realized that he was getting more serious about the relationship than she wanted. After he offered his help with her family history research, Sister Ritter finally gained the courage to tell him, "I don't mind you helping me search my family tree, but don't get any ideas about starting any new branches."

While vacationing in Jerusalem, Brother Ashcroft became acquainted with a hotel clerk. After four days, he boasted to this clerk, "One of my ancestors signed the Declaration of Independence."

"Congratulations, indeed," said the Jewish clerk. "One of mine signed the Ten Commandments!"

The second Sunday that Sister Lee taught the Family Research class, she made this comment: "Those who say the past cannot be changed have not yet written their personal history."

The following statements are requests sent to the Family History Department of the LDS Church. These are supposed extracts from real letters:

1. I would like to find out if I have any living relatives or dead relatives or ancestors in my family.
2. He and his daughter are listed as not being born.

3. My grandfather died at the age of 3.
4. We are sending you 5 children in a separate envelope.
5. The wife of #22 could not be found. Somebody suggested that she might have been stillborn— what do you think?
6. I am mailing you my aunt and 3 of their children.
7. Enclosed please find my Grandmother. I have worked on her for 30 years without success.
8. Now see what you can do. This family had 7 nephews that I am unable to find. If you know who they are, please add them to the list.
9. We lost our Grandmother; will you please send us a copy?
10. A 14-year-old boy wrote: "I do not want you to do my research for me. Will you please send me all of the material on the Welch line, in the U.S., England and Scotland countries?"

FOOD STORAGE
(A YEAR'S SUPPLY)

Members of the Church are counseled to get out of debt, live within their incomes, save a little, and have on hand enough food and clothing to survive for a year. The following items are the lighter side of food storage.

Sister Wright was speaking with her neighbor about food storage. She remarked, "We used to have a year's supply of food—until John came off his mission last month and ate it!"

"These used to be grapes," a grandmother explained to her 3-year-old grandson as she handed him some raisins that she just opened from her food storage pantry.

Staring at them intently, he said, "Really? What did you do, put 'em in the microwave?"

While looking at bottled water in their food storage room, an 8-year-old informed his mother, "It's too late to drink this. It says 'spring water,' and it's already summer."

Brother Amos decided it was time to go on a diet when his little son patted his tummy and innocently said, "Dad, is this what the Bishop means by a year's supply of food?"

A 6-year-old boy was working diligently with his grandfather; they were picking up potatoes out of the garden to store some away for food storage. Finally tiring of the whole project, the lad asked, "Grandpa, why did you bury these things anyway?"

One busy Saturday, Sister Tyler was leaving for work, while her husband was leaving for the temple. Their 11-year-old son asked them who was going to fix his breakfast.

Sister Tyler told him that his 15-year-old brother would. He quickly replied, "Would this be a good time to use my 72-hour kit?"

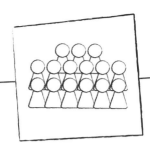

GENERAL AUTHORITIES

It has always been apparent that Apostles and Prophets are men with a very alert and pleasing sense of humor. Here is a collection of sayings from some of the Church's most witty leaders, past and present.

PRESIDENT HEBER C. KIMBALL

Heber C. Kimball was ordained an Apostle on February 14, 1835, at age 33. He was sustained as First Counselor to President Brigham Young on December 27, 1847, and he died June 22, 1868, in Salt Lake City, Utah.

The following story was related by Elder Orson F. Whitney, of the Quorum of the Twelve Apostles:

"Many years ago, on a hot and sleepy day, President Daniel H. Wells [who was the Second Counselor to President Brigham Young] was speaking from this stand, and right behind him, fast asleep, sat President Heber C. Kimball.

"As soon as Brother Wells had concluded his discourse, President Young tapped Brother Kimball on the shoulder, woke him, and asked him to be the succeeding speaker. President Kimball arose, and the first words he uttered were: 'I bear testimony to the truth of all that Brother Wells has said. I did not hear it, but I have full confidence in the man.'" (Conference Report, April 4, 1910, p. 85)

PRESIDENT DANIEL H. WELLS

Daniel H. Wells was set apart as Second Counselor to President Brigham Young on January 4, 1857, at age 42. Brother Wells was released at the death of President Young on August 29, 1877 and was sustained as a counselor to the Twelve Apostles on October 6, 1877. He died March 24, 1891, in Salt Lake City, Utah, at age 76.

The following letter was written by President Heber J. Grant, seventh President of the Church:

"May 1, 1935
"Dear Brother: . . .
"Never mind about being ugly. Abraham Lincoln has been referred to by some as the ugliest man that ever lived. The story goes that on one occasion he met my father-in-law, Daniel H. Wells, [who also was a statesman] and said to him, 'Wells, prepare to die. I have sworn that if I ever met an uglier man than myself, I would shoot him.'

"Daniel H. Wells is reported to have said, 'Shoot, Abe,—if I am uglier than you, I want to die.'"

(First Presidency Letterbooks, LDS Church Archives—CR 1 20, Film Reel #89, p. 480.)

ELDER J. GOLDEN KIMBALL

J. Golden Kimball was born June 9, 1853, in Salt Lake City, Utah. He was a son of President Heber C. Kimball.

He was sustained as one of the First Seven Presidents of the Seventy on April 5, 1892. Elder Kimball was killed in an automobile accident on September 2, 1938, near Reno, Nevada, at age 85.

Many people refer to Elder Kimball as "The Swearing Apostle."

This is an incorrect statement, for he was never called to serve in the Quorum of the Twelve Apostles, serving only as one of the First Seven Presidents of Seventy.

James Kimball, a relative who has often portrayed the life of Elder Kimball on stage, wrote the following: "I believe Uncle Golden was largely misunderstood. Many people remember him as a swearing Mormon elder who told jokes. He never told a joke in his life. Golden only made amusing observations about the ironies of Mormon life. He had an unvarnished, spontaneous wit."

Here are some of his classic statements.

"Remember when the sons of God got together and shouted for joy because they were coming to this earth life—

"If I had known then what I know now, I wouldn't have shouted so loud!"

"'People say I shouldn't swear. I don't mean to, brothers and sisters. It just comes out. They're left over from my cowboy days. That experience made me as tough as a pine knot. You can't drive mules if you can't swear. It's the only language they understand. I do swear a little, but they're just small leftovers from a far larger vocabulary!'"

"'My father was a wonderful man, a great Church leader. He had 43 wives, 46 sons and 22 daughters. He never mentioned any of these figures to Mother, and neither did I.'"

In April 1883, Golden was sent to the Southern States Mission. He said:
"It was a scant 18 years after the Civil War. Feelings still ran high against carpet-bagging Yankees, and Mormon missionaries were sometimes beaten, tarred and feathered, or even killed . . ."
"As a missionary, Golden is quoted as saying, 'I didn't know much about the Gospel. As a matter of fact, when I left on my mission I was a complete ignoramus. I thought epistles were wives of the apostles.'

"The Gospel must be true or greenhorn missionaries, like me, would have ruined it a long time ago."

The Rev. Charles A. Weatherbee was a popular Baptist minister who went throughout the Deep South spreading lies about the Mormons.

Golden encountered him as a young elder in Memphis, Tennessee. He and his companion were walking down the street, and coming from the other direction was Rev. Weatherbee . . . As Weatherbee got nearer, he recognized the two ragtag young men in ill-fitting suits carrying valises as Mormon elders. Righteous wrath suddenly darkened the minister's features. "Good morning, you sons of the Devil," he growled.

Golden doffed his hat politely and said, "Good morning, father!"

Near the end of his life, Golden was discussing the principal of revelation with a friend.

He reflected back on his reckless cowboy days and said, "When the Lord calls an old cowboy-muleskinner like me to be a General Authority, brother, I tell you it has to be revelation."

[The statements about and by J. Golden Kimball are used by permission from the book "J. Golden Kimball Stories: Mormonism's Colorful Cowboy" by James Kimball, Whitehorse Books, 1999.]

PRESIDENT JOSEPH FIELDING SMITH

Joseph Fielding Smith was ordained an Apostle on April 7, 1910, at age 33. He was ordained and set apart as President of the Church on January 23, 1970, at age 93. He died on July 2, 1972, in Salt Lake City, at age 95.

A lesser-known aspect of President Smith's personality is his sense of humor. The following examples are from a book written by a grandson, Joseph F. McConkie entitled "True and Faithful: The Life Story of Joseph Fielding Smith."

"On one occasion President Smith returned from a conference assignment in California with a lunch sack filled with olives he had picked. Delighted with his treasure, and always anxious to share, he asked one of his brethren if he had ever 'tasted an olive right off the tree.' His unsuspecting victim had not, so he took a healthy bite into one of the olives. This proved to be a rather bitter experience, and as the brother's face puckered up, President Smith asked innocently, 'What's the matter, did you get a bad one? Here, you had better try another one.'"

"At the conclusion of a stake conference, a man came up to President Smith, handed him the conference program and asked him if he would put his 'John Henry' on it. So President Smith did just that. In big bold letters he wrote JOHN HENRY."

"On a beautiful sunny holiday, one of President Smith's sisters went to visit him only to find him busily working in his office. Concerned that he was working too heard, she scolded him for not taking the day off. He responded, 'All my days are off.' Ignoring this, she continued: 'Now, I want you to go home and take a nap. George Albert Smith, Stephen L. Richards, and J. Reuben Clark always did, so you can too.'

"'Yes,' came the quick response, 'and look where they are now.'"

"In teaching his children, President Smith often told them that 'wickedness never was happiness' and that the adversary would rather have one of his children than someone else's because of their name. He would add with a chuckle, 'In the beginning all men were 'Smiths,' and when they did something wrong they had to change their name.'"

ELDER MATTHEW COWLEY

Matthew Cowley was ordained an Apostle on October 11, 1945, at age 45. He died December 13, 1953, at Los Angeles, California, at age 56.

Elder Cowley was recognized as a man of great faith. Here is an inspiring, humorous story from his ministry.

"I've told the story about the little baby nine months old who was born blind. The father came up with him on Sunday and said, 'Brother Cowley, our baby hasn't been blessed yet, and we'd like you to bless him.'

"I said, 'Why have you waited so long?'

"Oh, we just didn't get around to it.'

"Now, that's the native way; I like that. Just don't get around to doing things. Why not live and enjoy it. I said, 'All right, what's the name?' So he told me the name, and I was just going to start when he said, 'By the way, give him his vision when you give him a name. He was born blind.'

"Well, it shocked me, but then I said to myself, why not? Christ said to His disciples when He left them, 'Greater things than I have done shall you do.' And I had faith in that father's faith.

"After I gave that child its name, I finally got around to giving it its vision. That boy's about twelve years old now. The last time I was back there I was afraid to inquire about him. I was sure he had gone blind again.

"That's the way my faith works sometimes. So I asked the Branch President about him.

"He said, 'Brother Cowley, the worst thing you ever did was to bless that child to receive his vision. He's the meanest kid in this neighborhood. Always getting into mischief.'

"'Boy, I was thrilled about that kid getting into mischief!'"

(Address to the Brigham Young University Studentbody, Miracles, Wednesday, February 18, 1953.)

ELDER MARION G. ROMNEY

Marion G. Romney was ordained an Apostle on October 11, 1951, at age 54. He served for many years as a counselor in the First Presidency to LDS church presidents Harold B. Lee and Spencer W. Kimball.

After President Kimball's death, he resumed position in the Quorum of the Twelve Apostles and became President of the Quorum of the Twelve Apostles on November 10, 1985. He died May 20, 1988, at Salt Lake City, Utah, at age 90.

The following was related by Elder Romney:

"President Wilkinson, members of the faculty, and brothers and sisters in the audience, students—I am sorry that these lights do not permit me to see you, but I believe you are there.

"I am going to say something now very indiscreet. I understand that these services are being televised, and they will be shown again.

"I would like to advise the operators of the cameras to keep their cameras off the people on the row behind me who go to sleep. I say that advisedly because I watch quite regularly the re-showing of the devotional exercises of the BYU, and I am rather pleased that they cannot tape the audience."

(LEARN BY FAITH, an address given to the Brigham Young University Summer Studentbody, June 18, 1968, p. 1-2.)

PRESIDENT HUGH B. BROWN

Hugh B. Brown was ordained an Apostle on April 10, 1958, at age 74. He served as a counselor to President David O. McKay, and then resumed his position in the Quorum of the Twelve Apostles after President McKay's death in 1970.

Elder Brown passed away December 2, 1975, in Salt Lake City, Utah, at age 92.

While serving in the First Presidency, Elder Brown spoke at "Eternal Values Night," in Ricks College's Kirkham Auditorium on February 20, 1968. Here is a portion of that talk.

"Now, for fear that you are going to become to serious, let me tell you a quick story . . . I spent ten years in England and I learned something of the people and I learned to love them. The one thing I noticed was their sense of humor is quite different from ours.

"In fact, they do not understand our jokes very often and when they do it is usually crosswise. It is alleged that a certain Englishman was in Salt Lake City sometime ago. He was sitting alone in the rotunda of the Hotel Utah [now the Joseph Smith Memorial Building]. The clerk on duty thought he ought to go over and try to become friends with the fellow.

"He sat down by the Englishman and tried a joke on him. He said, 'You know, my mother had a baby. It was not my sister and it was not my brother. Who do you think it was?'

"The Englishman replied, 'I wouldn't know.'

"'Well,' the clerk said, 'it was me!'

"'That's jolly clever,' was the Englishman's response. When he went back to England he tried to tell it to a large audience. He said, 'You know, my mother had a baby. It was not my sister and it was not my brother. Who do you jolly-well think it was?' The audience did not know. 'It was the clerk down at Hotel Utah.'

"You see, sometimes they do not get the point."

Commenting about this story, Elder Brown then explained:

"I wonder if you think it is improper for me to engage in this sort of humor, whether or not humor has a place in a sacred meeting such as this. I remember what [Elder J.] Golden Kimball said when he came down to the stake where I was presiding. I introduced him as the 'Will Rogers' of the Church and told the audience that he was a great humorist. He said, 'You know, I think the Lord must like a joke. If he didn't he wouldn't have made some of you folks!'"

PRESIDENT SPENCER W. KIMBALL

Spencer W. Kimball was ordained an Apostle on October 7, 1943, at age 48. He was ordained and set apart as President of the Church on December 30, 1973, at age 78. He died November 5, 1985, in Salt Lake City, Utah, at age 90.

"After having throat surgery, Elder Kimball was allowed to use his voice, so long as he did not strain it or subject it to fatigue.

"But he had still not spoken at a conference with his gruff, unfamiliar voice, and he feared the experience. . ."

"Elder Delbert L. Stapley, the appointed conference visitor, offered him a chance to speak. Elder Kimball was tempted to pass the opportunity by, but he decided that if ever he were to speak in public again he would have to brave a first time. He started by telling the congregation that he had gone to New York and fallen among cutthroats and thieves who had slit his throat and stolen his voice. The audience laughed heartily and both he and they relaxed."

(Spencer W. Kimball, Twelfth President of The Church of Jesus Christ of Latter-day Saints, Bookcraft, 1977, pp. 310-311.)

The following story was related by President Spencer W. Kimball when he was President of the Quorum of the Twelve Apostles:

"President Bentley told you that I was born in another century; he didn't tell you which one. Last week—somewhere—I go so far and so often I can't remember what the last stake was, but a mother was showing her little girl the visitor to the conference and she said to her, 'Now you see, that is Brother Kimball, and he is one of Jesus' apostles,' and the little one looked up and said, 'Has he been here that long?'"

(An Address, September 26, 1971, BYU Ten Stake Fireside Address, p. 1.)

PRESIDENT BOYD K. PACKER

Boyd K. Packer was ordained an Apostle on April 9, 1970, at age 45. He was set apart as Acting President of the Quorum of the Twelve Apostles on June 5, 1994, and again March 12, 1995.

The following was from an Address he gave when he was an Assistant to the Quorum of the Twelve Apostles.

"Did you know that it is normal and healthy to be depressed occasionally? If you happen to hit a good sorry mood once in a while, relax and enjoy it—it is a good sign that you are normal.

"I really was hesitant to put this 'literature' in here, but it has a thought:

"If you can smile when things go wrong
"And say it doesn't matter,
"If you can laugh off cares and woe
"And trouble makes you fatter,
"If you can keep a cheerful face
"When all around are blue,
"Then have your head examined, bud,
"There's something wrong with you.
"For one thing I've arrived at:
"There are no ands and buts,
"A guy that's grinning all the time
"Must be completely nuts."
                        (Smile, Darned You, Smile.)

("LET NOT YOUR HEART BE TROUBLED . . ." An Address given to the Brigham Young University Student Body, October 4, 1966, p. 6.)

The following excerpts are from a book by President Packer entitled "Teach Ye Diligently" in which he writes, "To have a sense of humor is a lesson a teacher must learn. I have known teachers who did not learn it." In writing of humor in the classroom, he relates the following stories:

"A fellow seminary teacher had a good rebuttal to a student who said he didn't like school and wished it were out. [The teacher answered:] 'You should feel bad. I have to stay her till I'm sixty-five!'"

"Sometimes teachers are misunderstood, like the girl who complained that her Sunday School teacher had called her a 'dirty elephant.' Her irate parents got the bishop and the Sunday School teacher together, and when they finally had resolved the problem, they found that the teacher had told the daughter she was a 'disturbing element' in the class."

"I suppose every teacher has been misquoted and perhaps misrepresented and misunderstood in a lesson, and you have to learn to take that without complaint and be philosophical about it. It's like the account of the man who said to his wife, 'Did you hear the story of the window that needed cleaning?' The wife said, 'No, tell it to me.'
'Well, I guess I won't; you couldn't see through

it anyway,' was his reply. The woman, thinking that was a clever joke, told her neighbor, 'Have you heard the joke about the window you couldn't see through?'

'No,' was the reply. 'Well, it is too dirty to tell.'"

"I don't like the teacher;
"The subject is too deep.
"I'd quit this class
"But I need the sleep."

"Here is another lesson, drawn from a little girl who reported to her mother that her brother was setting traps for birds. She didn't like that at all. 'He won't catch any birds in his trap, will he, Mother?' she asked.

"The mother said, 'Perhaps he will—you cannot be sure he will not.'

"'I have prayed about it and asked Heavenly Father to protect the birds,' the girl said. Then, becoming more positive, she said, 'I know he won't catch any because I have prayed about it.'

"The mother asked, 'How can you be so positive?'

Then came the meaningful reply: 'He won't catch any birds because after I said my prayers, I went out and kicked those old traps all to pieces.'"

(Teach Ye Diligently, Deseret Book, 1975, pp. 135, 212-215.)

GODHEAD

As members of the LDS Church, we often recite the First Article of Faith. It is: "We believe in God, the Eternal Father, and in His Son, Jesus Christ, and in the Holy Ghost."

We honor and revere the members of the Godhead, and trust they have a sense of humor.

While riding in the family car one clear summer night, a 3-year-old daughter gazed intently at the star-studded sky. "Heavenly Father is home," she exclaimed. "All His lights are on."

A family who owned a large wheat and barley farm was in the middle of combining when they heard a weather forecast for rain and hail to be coming. The next day, however, there was blue skies and sunshine.

"Boy," their 5-year-old son commented, "I'm sure glad that Heavenly Father didn't listen to the weatherman."

While serving as a missionary, Elder Jones and his companion were speaking with an investigator at their first meeting. Trying to determine what this investigator knew, Elder Jones asked, "Do you know the name of God?"

After thinking about it, this man answered, "I believe his name is Andy!"

Shocked by this answer, Elder Jones asked, "How did you come up with that?"

"When I was younger, my family attended this church and the congregation would sing this song, "Andy walks with me, Andy talks with me."

While at her grandmother's home, a 5-year-old noticed some skywriting. Having been taught that Heavenly Father can communicate to his children on earth in various ways, this granddaughter asked her grandmother, "Is God writing to us?"

Having played hard all day, a young girl was really tired. While kneeling by her bed, with her mother by her side, this daughter said out loud, "Heavenly Father, I am just too tired to talk tonight—could you just remember one of my old prayers?"

One stormy day, a granddaughter, age 4, listened to the thunder rumble across the sky. She turned to her grandmother and asked sincerely, "Is Heavenly Father setting off fireworks in Heaven?"

A grandson, age 3, watched the weather go from rainy to sunny to rainy again within minutes. "Grandma," he curiously asked, "does Heavenly Father use a remote control?"

While hurrying through dressing, a 5-year-old son sometimes puts his shirt on the wrong way. One dark foggy morning, he looked out the window and proclaimed to his parents, "Heavenly Father put the sky on inside out today!"

In Primary, Sister Crane asked her class to draw a picture from one of the stories in the Bible. After several minutes passed, she walked around the room and observed what the students were drawing. She looked intently at Ryan's picture and asked what he was drawing. He replied, "This is a picture of Jesus."

Sister Crane kindly said, "I don't believe we know exactly what Jesus looks like."

Ryan seriously answered, "We will when I get through."

Two active boys, age 8, kept running up and down the hall of Church, yelling at one another, and disrupting classes. The Primary President had told them several times to be quiet and to go into their class. Having no success at controlling the boys, the Primary President finally told the Bishop about them. The Bishop found them and told the two to march down the hall to his office.

On their way, one boy whispered to his friend, "I'll go in and talk to him first. If what we have done is really bad, I'll jump-up and run out of his office. When you see me coming, you run too, and we will meet behind the Church. If it isn't too serious, I'll smile and wink at you, and you know all is okay."

At the office, the one said, "Can I come in first?"

The Bishop nodded his head in approval.

After the boy was seated, the Bishop asked, "Why are you making so much noise in the Church?"

"I don't know."

"Why didn't you do what the Primary President asked?"

Again he answered, "I don't know."

Trying to teach a lesson, the Bishop said, "This is Jesus' Church, and in His building, we are to be quiet and reverent."

After pausing, he continued, "If you are reverent in his Church, Jesus will be here. So, do you know where Jesus is?"

Startled, the boy said, "No!"

"You know it is embarrassing to your teacher and your mom and dad when you act like this. So, again I ask, do you know where Jesus is?"

At this question, this boy jumped up and ran out

of the office, grabbing his friend by the hand and said, "Run."

They didn't stop until there were safely hidden in the trees behind the Church. The other boy asked, "What happened?"

"This is serious. Jesus is missing, and they think we did it!"

Though this story is not true, the following joke began when President David O. McKay was the President of the Church. Since that time it has been attributed with each President of the Church, including President Gordon B. Hinckley.

One day President Hinckley said to his chauffeur, "Instead of you driving today, let me drive the limo, and you sit in the back seat of the car." Because the President requested this, the chauffeur readily complied.

President Hinckley was having so much fun driving that he forgot how fast he was going. A Highway Patrol officer soon spotted this speeding car and hurried to catch up to it. He turned on his flashing lights and siren. President Hinckley hurried off the road and put on the brakes. The Highway Patrol officer got out of his vehicle and walked slowly to the car President Hinckley was driving.

President Hinckley rolled down the tinted window and said hello to the officer. The officer immediately recognized him and said, "How are you today, President Hinckley? Did you know that you were driving faster than the posted speed limit?"

"I really wasn't paying any attention; but I believe you."

The patrol officer said, "Please wait here, while I check something in my patrol car." Inside his car, the officer called his superior officer and said, "You won't believe who I just picked up for speeding; it is President Gordon B. Hinckley. What should I do?"

"President Hinckley, the President of the LDS Church?" his superior asked.

"Yes, it is definitely President Hinckley."

"Well, he was speeding, right?"

"Yes."

"Well, then I guess you should give him a ticket."

The Highway Patrol officer replied, "I don't dare give him a ticket. If President Hinckley is driving the limo, who do you think is sitting in the back seat?"

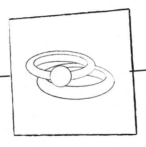

MARRIAGE
(DATING)

Paul, the apostle, wrote: "Marriage is honourable in all . . . . (Hebrews 13:4) Many scriptures speak of marriage of a man to a woman. (See Topical guide, LDS Bible Dictionary, pp.311-312) The Lord has declared in our day: "Thou shalt love thy wife with all thy heart, and shalt cleave unto her and none else." (D&C 42:22) Baptism is the gate to the celestial kingdom, while celestial marriage is the gate to exaltation in the highest heaven within the celestial world. These are conditioned on individuals remaining faithful to the end of their mortal life.

Here's a look at the lighter side of marriage.

My parents, Edward and Shirley Dana, have been married for 61 years. My father has always had a witty sense of humor. Three years ago, when Dad was 86, he bore his testimony and quipped, "They say if you have a disagreement with your wife, you should never go to sleep until it is resolved. I want you to know that I didn't sleep for the first three years of our marriage."

When I was about to marry, my Dad gave me this short, fatherly advice, "Just know that love is blind—but marriage is the eye-opener."

After dating a young woman two times, a returned missionary said to her, "I love you. Will you marry me? I know there can be no other for me."

Surprised by his words, the young woman replied, "I'm sorry, but I don't love you. You'll find some other girl, a beautiful girl."

Desperate, the returned missionary pleaded, "Please understand. I don't want a beautiful girl—I want you!"

Speaking with the Young Women of his ward about finding a good husband to marry, Brother Reynolds, a married man, and an Army recruiting officer, handed each girl a paper, and asked them to think about the typed message:

Marry a veteran, girls.
He can cook, make beds, is in perfect health
And, he is already used to taking orders.

The rented movie was sad, and the college coed sat there with tears streaming down her cheeks. Her date, a returned missionary, volunteered to help, "I'll kiss those tears away."

After she nodded her head in approval, the

returned missionary did his best, but the coed's tears still flowed.

He finally asked, "Will nothing stop your tears?"

"Not really," she said softly, "It's hay fever, but please go on with your treatment."

"I don't think that I'm being too picky," said the pretty, young woman to her mother, Sister Bell. "All I want is a nice man who loves and understands me. Is that too much to expect from a millionaire?"

A good friend of mine, Brother John Brockbank, told me that he gave this advice to his daughters, "You can marry a rich man just as easily as you can a poor one."

Two young women who attended the same single's ward were talking with one another. Sarah said, "I hear Derrick proposed to you. Did he happen to mention that he proposed to me first?"

Trying not to show her surprise, Monica replied, "Not specifically. However, he did say that he had done some foolish things before he met me."

Giving advice to her daughter who was quite serious with a young man, Sister Millet quoted this clever saying, "Never kiss behind the gate. Love is blind, but neighbors ain't."

During a college basketball game, a returned missionary said to his girlfriend, "Look at that tall fellow out there playing center, he'll be our best man before the season's over."

The young coed replied, "Oh, sweetheart, what a wonderful way to propose."

Brother Simmons was giving advice to his newly married son, who had been a good athlete in high school, "Man can climb the highest mountain, swim the widest river, do well at physical sports, but once he's married—he mostly takes out the garbage."

Sister Miles said to her attractive granddaughter, "Cindy, your mother has told me that you date a lot. Why are you not yet engaged to get married?"

Cindy replied sincerely, "I seem to suffer from Bible-itis. Men with their lips draw near to me, but their hearts are far from me."

A returned missionary said to his attractive date, "If I want to kiss you, will you yell for help?"

She replied, "Only if you think you need help."

Brother Cox was visiting with his new son-in-law and teased, "Just know that behind every successful man stands a surprised father-in-law."

Engaged to be married, a returned missionary asked his father, "How much does a marriage license cost?"

Brother Sorenson quipped, "Twenty dollars down and your income for the rest of your life."

Discussing married life with his married sons, Brother Lowder explained, "You'll know when the honeymoon is over when you telephone your wife to say you'll be home late for dinner, and your wife has already left a note on the table saying it's in the refrigerator."

Brother and Sister Wolfe were talking about their marriage of twenty years. She asked, "Are you going to stay with me when my hair is silver?"

Gently grasping her hands in his, Brother Wolfe responded. "I don't know why not?" I've been with you through all the other colors."

Sister Hansen was speaking with her neighbor about birthday gifts for their husbands. She said, "I got a set of golf clubs for my husband."

The neighbor responded, "Wow, I wonder how much I can get for my husband?"

At a family reunion, various male cousins were discussing married life.

Brother Long, who has been married for ten years, revealed this information: "Before a man gets married, he lies awake in bed all night thinking what his beloved said. Then, after they are married, he generally falls asleep before his beloved has finished saying it."

At a single adult fireside, the guest speaker gave this advice to the young men, "Be wise in who you decide to marry. Remember that some young women are like bathtubs—they acquire one ring after another."

Speaking in a combined Relief Society and Priesthood meeting, Brother Trippler remarked, "In marriage, we should do good turns for each other. In my marriage, I have learned this great truth: A husband soon learns that one good turn—will generally get the whole blanket."

During an interview with her ward Bishop, the single adult representative volunteered this information: "I've been asked to marry hundreds of times."

"Oh, who asked you?"

"My mother and father," she replied.

Elder J. Golden Kimball is attributed to saying many humorous things. Whether or not the following stories are true, they sound like something he might say.

During the course of his remarks to a group of young adults, Elder Kimball said, "I'm reminded that this is the month of June and that it is the marrying month. I suppose some of you young people will be getting hitched up to each other.

"I just want to warn you not to expect too much of each other, and then maybe you will not be disappointed. Now, when I got married, I thought I was marrying an angel, and many are the times since I wish I had."

and

"Some men select a girl because she has pretty eyes; some because she has pretty hair. I knew a man who chose a girl because she could sing.

"He married this gal, and the next morning when he saw her without any paint or powder on, and saw a part of her hair on the dresser, he looked at this gal and said, 'Sing, for heavens sake, sing!'"

MISSIONARY
(MISSION PRESIDENT)

Every member of the Church is a missionary, with the responsibility of teaching the gospel by word and deed to Heavenly Father's children. Full-time missionaries serve from 18 months to two years, without financial help from the Church, devoting their time to proclaiming the message of the restoration.

During this time, there are naturally a few humorous moments that are unforgettable.

When the Missionary Training Center was built in Provo, Utah, several years ago, athletic fields were built nearby so the missionaries would have a place to exercise in good weather.

However, the fields were so inviting that BYU students couldn't resisting playing touch football and throwing Frisbees on these fields. To deal with the problem, a large banner was posted which read: "Only For Missionaries."

The next day, some BYU students posted a new banner, which read: "Every member a missionary."

When a Priest Advisor took a group of young men for a visit to the Missionary Training Center in Provo, Utah, the elder at the desk handed each of the boys a descriptive pamphlet. One of the newly ordained priests glanced through the pamphlet and gasped, "This must be a mistake. It says that the missionaries rise each morning at 6 a.m."

The elder at the desk smiled and said, "It's definitely a mistake, but it's true!"

In a missionary training class at an Institute of Religion, the instructor was advising the young men to begin focusing on their forthcoming missions, rather than on girlfriends that some might have.

After explaining that there was a time and a place for everything, the instructor said that marriage would eventually come to those who served an honorable mission.

To lighten the seriousness of the lesson, the teacher taped a large poster on the chalk board. On it was written this message: "Lord, please bless the Laurel girls. They will be the right age when I get home."

In Rome, two missionaries visited the Vatican. Pointing to the ceiling, a guide told them, "It took Michelangelo four years to get that ceiling painted."

The junior companion turned to his companion and replied, "He must have had the same landlord we have now."

At his missionary farewell, Jim said, "I think it is important to tell you that our Bishop has strived to get the Priest-age boys in our ward to serve a mission. For instance, he asked the most handsome one to go, and he turned him down.

"Then, he asked the most intellectual one to go, and he turned him down.

"So, he asked the one with the most potential to go, and he turned him down.

"Not being discouraged, our Bishop decided to ask me. As you can see, I decided to accept the call of the Lord to serve a mission.

"After all, how could I turn the Bishop down after he asked me the fourth time?"

When parents were allowed to see a missionary leave from the Salt Lake Airport, a family visited with their missionary who was called to serve in South America. Concerned for his health, Sister Ivins put her arms around her boy and said, "Now son, don't eat the food or drink the water."

Flying over Portland, Oregon in the early evening to begin my missionary labors in the Northwestern States Mission, I looked out the window of the plane at thousands of lights shining down below and my heart sunk. I said to myself, "I have to knock on every one of those doors?"

A Catholic Priest went into a barber shop for a haircut. When he was finished, the barber refused to take payment saying, "You're a man of the cloth. This is a free service that I offer to you."

The Priest thanked the barber and went on his way. The next morning, the barber found a package from the Priest on his doorstep with two fishes and two loaves of bread inside.

The next week, a Jewish Rabbi went into this same shop for a haircut. Again the barber refused payment saying, "You're a man of God. This is a free service I offer to you."

The Rabbi thanked the barber and went on his way. The next morning, the barber found a package on his doorstep from the Rabbi with a beautiful Star of David inside.

The following week, two LDS missionaries went into this same shop for haircuts. Again, the barber refused payment saying, "You are in the service of God. This is a free service I offer to you."

The next morning, the barber found twelve missionaries on his doorstep.

At a mission office, several missionaries smiled as they read the Missionary Safety Slogan: "Remember, it's not only the car that can be recalled by its Maker."

A missionary serving in France received a package from some of his fraternity brothers in Arizona. It contained what appeared to be a very plain and ordinary necktie, suitable for wearing on a mission. This missionary wore it often. One evening, when he and his companion were visiting a very proper family, in the middle of a spiritual discussion, the lights suddenly went out. It was pitch black—except for the missionary's plain tie, on which gleamed in florescent colors the words: "KISS ME!"

An Idaho farm boy went on a mission to Indiana. He wrote a letter to his parents, "I sure am enjoying missionary life. It is really nice to lie in bed every morning until 6 a.m."

An investigator was explaining to the missionaries how challenging his life was. He said, "The stock market is down, my son broke his arm last week, and my wife's father is not expected to live much longer."

The junior companion replied, "You think you have problems. I just bought a suit with two pairs of pants, and yesterday I tore a hole in the suitcoat."

There were smiles in the congregation as the newly returned missionary stood up to give his report and began: "It's so go to be home and to see all of you: Dad and Mom, my little brothers, friends, former mission companions, my girlfriend—and her husband . . . ."

One evening, when my son Nathan was five, we talked about him going on a mission. Somehow thinking he would be leaving the next morning, he asked with a trembling voice, "Dad, when I go, will you come with me?"

A mission president was giving orientation to six new missionaries. During his remarks, he quipped, "When a big, mean dog chases after you, remember that you don't have to run faster than the dog—you just have to outrun your companion."

My first mission president is a wonderful man, Robert L. Backman. He later served as a member of the First Quorum of the Seventy.

Several years after being released as mission president of the Northwestern States Mission, he spoke in a Sacrament Meeting I attended. Elder Backman related an experience he had while serving as mission president. He said:

"It was the first day in the mission field for a missionary who had been raised on a dairy farm in western Utah. He was away from home for the first time. We had completed our orientation, and I found him crying in a corner of the dining room. I put my arm around him and asked if there was anything I could do. He turned, burying his head on my shoulder and said, 'Oh, President, I miss my cows.'"

(Used by permission)

Shortly after Elder Paul H. Dunn was released as the president of the New England Mission, he spoke in a stake conference I attended.

He said, "Someone asked me what it was like being a mission president. It was like taking two hundred Priests on an overnight hike for three years."

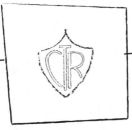

MORMONS

Mormon was an ancient Nephite prophet who abridged and compiled the sacred records of his people under the title "The Book of Mormon." Members of the LDS Church are often known by the nickname "Mormons," a name which is not offensive or objectionable to them. Mormons are true Christians.

The following stories share the lighter side of being a Mormon.

Two primary boys were talking about how good their fathers were. Tyler said, "My Dad is so good, he goes home teaching the first day of the month."

Kevin responded, "My Dad is better than that. He goes the day before that!"

For years, Church leaders have counseled the members of the Church not to gamble or play games of chance. Still, many members who live in Utah travel to Wendover, Nevada for that purpose.

Giving a lesson in his High Priest Group in Salt Lake City, Brother Dutson gave this illustration concerning some beliefs in the world:

"1. Muslims do not recognize the Jews as God's chosen people.

"2. Many Jews do not recognize Jesus as the Messiah.

"3. Protestants do not recognize the Pope as the leader of the Christian world.

"4. Mormons do not recognize each other in Wendover.

Years ago, a kindergarten teacher gave her class a "show and tell" assignment of bringing something to represent their religion. A boy stood in front of the class and said, "My name is Ben. I am Jewish and this is the Star of David."

Another boy stood in front of the class and said, "My name is Thomas. I am Catholic and this is a Crucifix."

Still another boy stood in front of the class and said, "My name is Johnny. I am Mormon and this is a casserole."

A Catholic Priest was walking down the street one day, when he saw a young boy in a yard sprinkling water on some newborn puppies.

The Priest turned to the boy and asked curiously,

"What are you doing?"

"I'm baptizing my new puppies."

The Priest asked, "What kind of puppies are they?"

The lad answered, "Catholic puppies."

Satisfied with this answer, the Priest continued his walk down the street.

A week later, the Priest noticed the same boy dunking his puppies gently in a small swimming pool. The Priest again asked, "What are you doing?"

"I'm baptizing my Mormon puppies," replied the lad.

"Aren't these the same puppies you said were Catholic puppies last week?"

"Yes," the boy answered. "But now their eyes are open!"

In the spirit of comedian Jeff Foxworthy's "You Might Be a Redneck" characterization, here is a list to show that you might be a Mormon.

1. If all of your dishes have your name written on them with masking tape—you might be a Mormon.

2. If you postdate your checks while shopping on Sunday—you might be a Mormon.

3. If your Mom was expecting a child at your sister's wedding reception—you might be a Mormon.

4. If you have never arrived at a Church meeting on time—you might be a Mormon.

5. If you pray that your food might "nourish and strengthen your body" before eating doughnuts—you might be a Mormon.

6. If you think Jell-O is one of the basic food groups—you might be a Mormon.

7. If at least one of your salad bowls is at a neighbor's house—you might be a Mormon.

8. If you have ever written a "Dear-John" letter to more than two missionaries on the same day—you might be a Mormon.

9. If you were frustrated when your son "only" got accepted to Harvard, instead of BYU—you might be a Mormon.

10. If you had one child in diapers and one on a mission—you might be a Mormon.

11. If you have more wheat stored in your basement than most Third World countries—you might be a Mormon.

12. If you have to guess more than five times the name of the child you're disciplining—you might be a Mormon.

13. If you go to a party and someone spikes the punch with Pepsi or Coke—you might be a Mormon.

14. If you arrive late to a Church activity and are the first person there—you might be a Mormon.

An acronym is formed from the initial letter or letters of each part of a compound term. With that stated, here's some sentences that only Mormons could decipher.

My son's a CTR . . . I go to PEC.

I work for CES . . . I study the TG.

I read the B of M . . . I probe the D&C.

I search the KJV . . . I ponder the JST.

Today in BYC . . . we planned for EFY.

I stayed a little later after . . . and had a PPI.

The YM and YW . . . are putting on a play.

It's one that I remember . . . we did in MIA.

Before our oldest son . . . went in the MTC,

he helped the BSA . . . complete their SME.

Soon our oldest daughter . . . is going for the Y.

Soon our oldest clothing . . . is going to the DI.

If you've understood . . . this alphabetic mess,

The chances are quite good . . . you are LDS.

Code:
    CTR= Choose the Right
    PEC= Priesthood Executive Committee
    CES= Church Educational System
    TG=Topical Guide
    B of M= Book of Mormon
    D&C= Doctrine and Covenants
    KJV= King James Version of the Bible
    JST= Joseph Smith Translation of the Bible
    BYC= Bishop Youth Counsel
    EFY= Especially For Youth
    PPI= Personal Priesthood Interview
    YM= Young Men
    YW= Young Women
    MIA= Mutual Improvement Association
    MTC= Missionary Training Center
    BSA= Boy Scouts of America
    SME= Sustaining Membership Enrollment
    Y= Brigham Young University
    DI= Deseret Industries
    LDS= Latter-day Saint

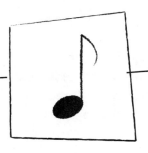

MUSIC

Through the Prophet Joseph Smith, the Lord revealed: "Praise the Lord with singing, with music, with dancing, and with a prayer of praise and thanksgiving." (D&C 136:28)

Inspirational music is an important part of divine worship. "For my soul delighteth in the song of the heart," the Lord says, "yea, the song of the righteous is a prayer unto me, and it shall be answered with a blessing upon their hearts." (D&C 25:12)

Good and uplifting music is given of God to further his purposes, and it is an important part of Sunday services.

♪

A young boy was sitting next to his mother in Sacrament meeting and whispered, "What is this man next to me singing?"

"Bass," she whispered back.

"That's why it sounds so funny. We're singing 'Silent Night.'"

♪

A ward chorister was speaking with the organist. He sighed, "Somehow this calling is not what I pictured when I was told in my patriarchal blessing that I would someday be the leader of many."

After their first ward choir practice, Brother Stowell said to his wife, "When I sing, what should I do with my hands?"
She replied, "Hold them over your mouth!"

A ward choir director was telling the choir members about his childhood. He explained, "When I was young, my mother would always sing 'Silent Night,' instead of a lullaby. Later, I found out it wasn't because that was her favorite song. She was silently praying that I would let her have one."

Sister Cooper had just turned 90. She had directed and sung in the ward choir for 50 years. At a social to honor her long-time music achievement, past and present members of the choir were invited. At this large gathering of people, the new choir director said to Sister Cooper, "All of us are willing to sing for you; therefore, please choose three hymns."
Sister Cooper thought for a moment. Then, she wittingly said (as she pointed her index in their direction), "I'll take him, and him, and him."

Here's another story from the time that J. Golden Kimball was president of the Southern States Mission.

"Golden attended a mission conference in the city of Mine Lick, Tennessee, in 1892. As mission president, Golden was there to preside.

"The missionaries of the Central Tennessee District decided at the last moment that they would present a hymn at this conference. By their own admission, their presentation of this hymn, unfortunately, rang both high and loud in certain parts.

"Golden arrived and heard the elders practicing— in fact, it was impossible not to. He stood there for several minutes listening. He then asked Elder Willard Bean, who was leading the singing, to step outside with him.

"When they got outside, he said, 'Now, Elder Bean, I think it best that we have you and the other missionaries sing in another room. We'll bore some holes in the door and let a little in at a time. You see, my eardrums can't take it all at once.'"

(More J. Golden Stories; by James Kimball, 2002, White Horse Books, pp. 95-96.)

♪

A ward music director's first name was Hope. She was a person who enthusiastically smiled and maintained eye contact with the congregation.

Hope was a petite little mother who was soon expecting another child. In fact, she was several weeks overdue and the ward members were anxiously awaiting the arrival of the new baby.

Every week, they expected to see a substitute

Stories and Jokes of Mormon Folks 121

choir director. On a particular Sunday, the Bishop had selected one of the ward's favorite hymns, "We thank thee, O God, for a prophet."

Suddenly while singing the song, the majority of the congregation burst into laughter as they sang this verse: "There is hope smiling brightly before us, and we know that de-liv-'rance is nigh."

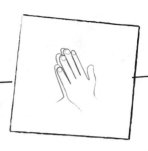

PRAYER

To pray is to speak with Heavenly Father, either vocally or by forming the thoughts in the mind. Prayer has been a part of the gospel from the beginning.

Prayers of the Latter-day Saints are expected to conform to a prescribed standard. They are to be addressed to the Father; should always be in the name of Jesus Christ; must be reverential and worshipful in nature; which includes the use of the pronouns thee and thine; and they should be closed with the word Amen.

Of course, there are exceptions. Here are some examples.

Having received permission from his parents, Bart invited two of his non-member friends to a barbeque party on a Saturday. When family and friends sat down to eat, one non-member boy turned to the other and said quietly, "They always say a blessing on the food. I think they do it so everyone has a fair start."

Timmy, age 8, had only heard his grandfather pray at Thanksgiving dinner or at special family gatherings, where he typically said a long prayer over the food.

One night after a fun campout and fishing trip, this grandfather—to Timmy's surprise—asked a brief blessing on the food.

With a gleam in his eye, Timmy said to his grandfather, "You don't pray so long when you're hungry, do you Grandpa?"

Sister Morgan, who is a math teacher at a local high school, was giving a lesson on prayer in Relief Society.

After giving various examples, she decided to share what was written on a sign in the faculty lounge of the school: "In case of terrorist attack, the Supreme Court's ruling on prayer will be temporarily suspended!"

Then, she made this comment, "No matter where you stand on the prayer-in-school issue, children will pray as long as they have to take math tests."

Giving a lesson on prayer, the Mia Maid teacher gave various examples from the scriptures. Then, she decided to tell of a prayer that one of her unmarried female cousins had said: "I ask nothing for myself, but my brother sure wants a brother-in-law."

The following was told by Elder J. Golden Kimball about his father, President Heber C. Kimball:

"I feel a good deal, I think, like my father did one time when he was praying. You know he was rather peculiar, and prayed in his own way.

"He was praying about someone, and he stopped in his prayer and laughed very heartily, and then said, 'O Lord, forgive me, it makes me laugh to pray about some men.'"

(Conference Report, October 8, 1905, p. 81.)

The following was related by Elder Bruce R. McConkie, then a member of the First Council of the Seventy:

"I recall an instance from early Church history, from the days of persecution and difficulties, Heber C. Kimball, then a member of the Council of Twelve, found himself in circumstances where he sought hospitality from a member of the Church, a widow woman.

She fed him what she had, bread and milk, and provided a room and a bed for him. He went to retire. She thought: 'Here's my opportunity, I would like to find out what an Apostle says when he prays to the Lord.' So after the door was closed, she crept quietly up to it to listen. She heard Brother Kimball sit down on the bed; she heard each of his shoes fall to the floor; she heard him lean back on the bed and then say these words: 'Oh Lord, bless Heber, he is so tired,' and that was it."

(An Address, October 28, 1966, Are the General Authorities Human, p. 1.)

When 5-year-old Josh was saying his evening prayer with his mother, he said: "Our Father who art in heaven, how do you know my name?"

After returning from his mission, Terry took his girlfriend to supper and to a show at a theater. After thanking her for going, he started to leave the front porch.

Sweetly, this girlfriend said, "Didn't you forget something?"

"Yes," he replied, "Let's have a word of prayer."

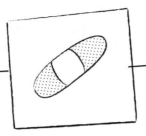

REPENTANCE
(SIN)

Repentance is the process whereby an individual is enabled to cast off the burden of guilt, wash away the filth of iniquity, and become clean and free from the bondage of sin.

To gain forgiveness through repentance a person must have a conviction of guilt, a godly sorrow for sin, and a contrite spirit.

Repentance is essential to salvation; without it no person who is accountable can be saved in the kingdom of God.

But everything isn't gloom and doom. Here are some lighter moments involving repentance.

Having a serious discussion with the Priests in his ward about sin and repentance, a Bishop asked the boys, "What must we do before we can expect forgiveness of our sins?"

One of the boys answered, "Sin!"

During a Family Home Evening lesson on repentance, an 11-year-old son asked innocently, "Dad, what does it mean when they say, 'Thou shalt not commit agriculture.'"

Not missing a beat, Brother Swan answered, "That just means that an individual shouldn't plow another man's field."

After visiting with her parents and her Bishop, Emily put the following advertisement in a college campus newspaper:

"Terry S, contact me immediately. Bring three rings: Engagement, Wedding, and Teething. Have news for you. Emily."

Sister Reynolds took her 10-year-old twin boys to a museum to look at the paintings. Several paintings showed individuals with halos above their head. Sister Reynolds explained that the halo meant those individuals were good people.

Then, she gave this gospel lesson: "Just know that if you commit sin, a halo only has to slip down a few inches to become a noose."

SCOUTS

The Aaronic Priesthood provides opportunities for young men to participate in service projects and activities designed to build religious faith, moral character, and physical fitness.

Most LDS young men also participate in the Boy Scout program during their early teenage years. The following stories share the lighter side of Scouting.

After having a physical game of tag football with twelve Scouts, one of the Scoutmasters was speaking with a counselor in the Bishopric. He quipped, "The trouble with being a Scoutmaster today is that you can't be sure whether the boys are following you or chasing you."

"What a fine-looking youngster," said the elderly gentlemen to Sister Scott. "While he's young, I hope you encourage him to be an Eagle Scout and to go on a mission."

"Yes," smiled the fond mother. "But I'm afraid it's

going to be difficult, since . . ."

"Oh, nonsense!" interrupted the older gentleman. "As the twig is bent, so is the tree inclined."

"I agree with that statement," the mother said. "However, this twig is bent on being a girl, and I am inclined to let her be just that!"

During a meeting of several Scoutasters from various stakes, a Stake President was commenting about the challenges and rewards of Scouting. Then, he made this observation: "Up to sixteen years of age, a lad is a Boy Scout. After that, he turns into a girl scout."

At a Scout social, Sister Whiting said, "Son, that's the fifth time you've been back for ice cream and cake. As a Scout, doesn't that embarrass you?"

"Why should it?" he answered. "I keep telling them it's for you."

After the Scouts had finished a day of hiking, they stopped at an ice cream shop to buy them a treat. Each of the boys quickly told the attendant what kind of ice cream they wanted. But when it came to Tony, the Scoutmaster told him, "I think you should have vanilla."

"Why?" asked Tony. "Chocolate is my favorite."

"Yes, I know," said the wise Scoutmaster, "but I think vanilla will look better on your uniform."

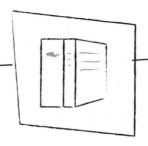

SCRIPTURES

The standard works of the Church are the following four volumes of scripture: The Bible, Book of Mormon, Doctrine and Covenants, and Pearl of Great Price.

These four volumes of scriptures are the will, mind, word, and voice of the Lord. (Eighth Article of Faith)

When the living oracles speak in the name of the Lord or are moved upon by the Holy Ghost, their words are considered scripture and are binding upon the Latter-day Saints.

The following are the lighter side of scriptures:

A Relief Society president was telling a class about the laws of God.

She explained that different people view different things in the Ten Commandments. She said, "Some people look for divine guidance, some for a code of living, and some—for loopholes."

A Primary teacher gathered the young boys and girls around her and told the story of Jesus feeding the multitude in the miraculous manner as told in the New Testament.

Going home that afternoon, one of the mothers, anxious to impress the lesson upon the mind of her little son, decided to talk to him about it.

"What did Sister James tell us today?" the mother asked.

The boy replied, "She told us how the Savior fed the people."

This mother asked, "How many people?"

"Five thousand," he replied.

"And what did he feed them with?"

"Five loaves of bread and two fishes."

"Well, now," said the mother, "how do you suppose Jesus could do that?"

The little boy thought for a moment and said, "Well, I don't believe those in the middle got any."

A Teacher Quorum instructor asked the boys, "Which of all the miracles that Jesus did, do you like best?"

One of the young men joked: "The one where everyone loafs and fishes."

Two college coeds were talking about their previous night's date. One explained what happened on her date with a returned missionary. She said, "The night was beautiful, the moon was so romantic and bright that you could read the scriptures."

The other asked anxiously, "What did your date do?"

"He read the scriptures."

The following story was told by Elder A. Theodore Tuttle, a member of the First Council of the Seventy, about Bruce R. McConkie, a member of the Quorum of Twelve Apostles who passed away in 1985.

Elder Tuttle said, "Some years ago, while Elder McConkie was still a member of the First Council of the Seventy, we were discussing why he was such an avid student of the gospel.

"He said, 'It was my father who first taught me the gospel and inspired me to study.' Imagine the loss to this church if a wise father had not taken the time to teach and inspire his son.

"Ever since those early days, Elder McConkie has been a constant student of the scriptures. . . . In those days there was a rumor going about the Church that Elder McConkie knew hundreds of scriptures from memory. Those of us in the First Council knew that was not so, and set about to correct the record. When people would say, 'Doesn't Elder McConkie know hundreds of scriptures?' We would say say, No, he does not. That's a falsehood. He only knows four scriptures: The Bible, the Book of Mormon, the Doctrine and Covenants, and the Pearl of Great Price!'"

(An Address, July 19, 1981, Provo Temple Workers Meeting, p. 10.)

Brother and Sister Mills had recently taken up jogging. On one morning, Brother Mills tried unsuccessfully to awaken his wife, who had been up several times during the night with a fussy baby.

Standing by their bed, Brother Mills said cheerfully, "The scripture says early to bed and early to rise . . . ."

Far from under the covers came the sleepy reply, "How do you know it has been translated correctly?"

TEENAGERS

Teenagers can be both a joy and a challenge to their parents. Thankfully they also provide a good source of entertainment.

Visiting with two of her neighbors about their teenage children, Sister Hawkes quipped, "Isn't it amazing how a teenager who can't learn to run a vacuum cleaner or a lawnmower quickly learns how to drive the family car?"

Sister Garrison was having a bit of a struggle with her teenage son. He continually came home later than the time they had agreed to, and she worried he was getting into trouble.

Sister Garrison finally told him, "Every time you do something wrong, I get another gray hair."

With a smile on his face, her son answered teasingly, "Is that why grandma's hair is so gray?"

After giving instructions to their teenage children, Brother and Sister Hatch were on their way out for the evening. The telephone rang so Brother Hatch returned and answered it.

He listened for a moment and then said into the phone, "How on earth would I know? Why don't you call the Coast Guard?"

Then he hung up the phone and started toward the front door.

"Who was that, dear?" Sister Hatch said.

"I haven't the faintest idea," he replied. "Some dumb teenager wanted to know if the coast was clear."

The Young Women Presidency was discussing the temptations the young women were facing in their lives.

One of the counselors said that when she was younger, she started to do things that concerned her parents. Then, her grandmother had said something to her one day that she had never forgotten; it was simple and clever.

Whenever she was tempted to be morally unclean, she remembered this saying: "One sure way of keeping a teenage daughter out of hot water—put some dirty dishes in it."

In a Relief Society meeting about families, the instructor was talking about the challenges of raising teenagers. One of the members raised her hand and said, "You can tell that a teenager is growing up when he stops asking where he came from and quits telling you where he's going!"

In a High Priest meeting, some grandfathers were concerned how much television was being watched by their teenage grandchildren after school.

One of the older High Priests wryly said, "There would be fewer problems with teenagers today if they had to chop wood to keep the TV going."

In a Laurel class, Sister Buttars was trying to teach the girls the value of repetition. "You can be assured that if you repeat something seven to ten times, it will be yours forever."

On the back row, one of the girls suddenly whispered, "Ryan, Ryan, Ryan . . . ."

While at a family reunion, Sister Cahoon told some of her relatives, "It seems that my teenage daughter can't find anything to wear in a closet full of clothes, and my teenage son can't find anything to eat in a refrigerator full of food."

A teenage daughter said, "Dad, the Bishop wants me to give a 15-minute talk in Sacrament Meeting next Sunday."

"That's great, dear."

"But Dad, I can't talk for 15 minutes."

Her father smiled and said, "Perhaps you can take your cell phone to the podium with you."

Talking with her visiting teacher about shopping with her teenage daughter, Sister Knowles said, "She's a girl with a great deal of faith."

"That's wonderful. Can you give me an example?"

Sister Knowles laughed. "Well, she believes she can fit a size 9 body in a size 7 dress."

Having turned 13 the week before, a teenager jokingly said to his father after Fast and Testimony Meeting, "Let's hurry home and celebrate the feast of the fast over."

Sister Long, who is an English teacher, was telling the Relief Society members how four high school boys, afflicted with spring fever, skipped her class. After lunch, they reported to her that their car had had a flat tire.

Much to their relief, I smiled and said, "Well, you missed the test this morning, so take your seats apart from one another and get a piece of paper."

Still smiling, I waited for them to settle. Then, I told them, "First question: 'Which tire was flat?'"

Giving a lesson on marriage, a Sunday school teacher tried to explain to the teenage group the significance of the color white.

"White," she said, "stands for purity and joy. That is why the bridal gown is white. Her wedding day should be the most pure and joyous occasion of a young lady's life."

One of the boys asked, "Why, then, does the husband wear a black tuxedo?"

Speaking with the girls and their parents about the girls going to summer camp in a week, Sister Krebs made this observation, "When girls leave for summer camp, it can be a highly emotional experience. Let me tell you about my teenage niece last year. She cried her eyes out when she suddenly realized that she was leaving those nearest and dearest to her—the phone, the TV, and the bathtub."

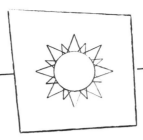

SUNBEAMS

In Junior Primary, the three-year-olds are called Sunbeams. Straight out of Nursery, they can sometimes be a handful, but also a source of delight. Here is a sampling of life as a Sunbeam.

One of the Primary songs is "Follow the Prophet." The seventh verse reads: "Jonah was a prophet, tried to run away, But he later learned to listen and obey. When we really try, the Lord won't let us fail: That's what Jonah learned deep down inside the whale."

With that information, the following story was related by Sister Chris Glad:

It was asked of the children what song they wanted to sing. A little girl raised her hand and said, "Swallow the Prophet."

A leader asked curiously, "What do you mean?"

The girl replied, "Jonah was a prophet, who was swallowed by a whale."

One of the Primary songs is "Jesus Wants Me for a Sunbeam." Sister Chris Glad also related this story:

In another Primary, it was asked of the children what song they wanted to sing. A Sunbeam girl raised her hand and said, "Jesus Wants Me for a Sardine."

The following was originally told by a physician in Utah:

I work part-time as a teacher of family doctors. The program provides training on psychiatric disorders and emphasizes the important of emotional support.

The new doctors are given plenty of time in clinics to visit their patients and learn about their challenges.

One of our interns, who has never lived in Utah and knows nothing about Mormons, is still struggling to understand the cultural climate here. He was interviewing a new patient and stumbled on what he thought was a raging psychosis. Here's a summary of his conversation with the patient.

Doctor: "Well, Mrs. Olsen, we've talked about your high blood pressure and your medications. Are you experiencing any particular stress in your life?"

Patient: "Oh, yes. It's the Sunbeams. They're driving me crazy."

Doctor: "The sunbeams?"

Patient: "Yes. I've never had trouble with them before, but this group won't sit still. They bounce all over the room, and run out the door and down the hall."

Doctor (reaching for a pen): "Have you told anyone about this?"

Patient: "Of course. I told the president."

Doctor: "Really! What did the president tell you?"

Patient: "She said Sunbeams are like that. I'm just going to have to learn to deal with them."

Doctor (concerned that he may be missing something): "I know people who are sensitive to sunbeams. Do they cause you a rash or anything?"

Patient: "A rash? No."

Doctor: "Then what is the biggest problem they're creating?"

Patient: "It's the noise. They just won't quit talking."

Doctor (astonished): "The sunbeams are talking to you?"

Patient: "Well, yes. But mostly they talk to each other."

Doctor (scribbling furiously in the chart): "I see. Can anyone else hear them talking?"

Patient (after a moment of stunned silence): "You're not LDS, are you?"

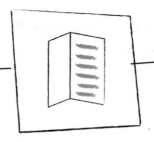

WARD NEWSLETTER BLUNDERS

Our opening song is "Angels We Have Heard Get High."

Don't let worry kill you—let the Church help.

Remember in prayer the many that are sick of our church and community.

For those of you who have children, and don't know it, we have a nursery downstairs.

Bishop Smith spoke briefly, much to the delight of his audience.

Homemaking this week will meet at 7 p.m.
The topic is weight management. Please use
the large double doors at the side entrance.

Eight new choir dresses are currently needed;
due to the addition of several new members,
and to the deterioration of some older ones.

Please join us as we show our support for
Amy and Alan in preparing for the girth of
their first child.

This morning, we are happy to announce the
birth of David Alan Smith, the sin of Brother
and Sister Julius Smith.

During the absence of our Bishop, we enjoyed
the rare privilege of hearing a good talk when
Brother Adams supplied our pulpit.

On a Fast Sunday, the opening
song was listed: "Because We
Have Been Given Mush."

THE WORD OF WISDOM

A revelation given to the Prophet Joseph Smith on February 27, 1833, contained a code of health commonly known as the Word of Wisdom.

Now found in D&C 89, it contains both positive and negative instructions. Three types of things are prohibited by the Word of Wisdom—tobacco, strong drinks, and hot drinks, with strong drinks meaning alcoholic beverages and hot drinks meaning tea and coffee.

The following stories share the lighter side of the Word of Wisdom.

In a Relief Society meeting, Sister Smart was counseling the sisters to limit foods that can cause harmful cholesterol. To emphasize her teaching, she turned over a large sheet of paper that was attached to a movable chalkboard. On this sheet of paper the following statement was written:

"Some Mormons are eating their way to the Cholesterol Degree of Glory."

While waiting to go to Sacrament Meeting, Brad, age 14, said to his 15-year-old sister, "To look at you, a person would think there was a famine in the land."

Rachel responded, "Yes, and to look at you, that same person would think you were the cause of it."

Sister Tripp and Sister Stuart were discussing the eating habits of their children. Sister Tripp quipped, "In our home, mealtime is the time of day when the kids sit down to the table to continue eating."

Having a discussion about their desires to be slender and healthy, Sister Pickens said to her three married granddaughters, "There is no guaranteed way to lose weight—although living on Social Security comes close."

Speaking with his sons about their eating habits, Brother Kipper remarked, "Did you know that nutritionists have proven that obesity is catching: You can get it from your knife, fork, and spoon."

While talking with her married daughters about homemaking skills, Sister Whitaker quipped, "I still have the first two loaves of whole wheat bread that I ever baked. I use them for book ends."

While on their honeymoon, Brother and Sister Walters went to a nice restaurant.

Brother Walters said to his bride, "Science says that what we eat, we will become."

Excited by that statement, Sister Walters seized the menu and said, "Wonderful. Let's order something rich!"

After catching two of his younger grandsons smoking, Brother Steele told them what his grandfather had said to him when he was caught smoking at a young age:

"Tobacco is a filthy weed.
"It's the devil that sows the seed.
"It stains your fingers and stinks your clothes,
    "And it makes a stove pipe of your nose."

One day in Gospel Doctrine class, the instructor became adamant that Church members should only eat natural foods. Brother Firth claimed that the preservatives in store-bought foods were against the Word of Wisdom.

At this comment, one of the older sisters in the ward raised her hand and said, "I disagree with what you say. Besides, I'm at an age when I'll have nothing to do with natural foods. I need all the preservatives I can get!"

Giving a lesson on the Word of Wisdom, a seminary teacher said to the class, "I would like to give you a demonstration on the harmful effects of drinking alcoholic beverages.

"Here are two glasses; one is filled with water, the other with whiskey. I will now place a worm in each glass. Notice how the worm in the water wiggles about in the water, but lives, while the worm in the whisky dies in agony. Now, students, what is the moral of this story?"

One of the boys jokingly said, "If you don't want worms, drink whiskey."

The following story was related by Elder Matthew Cowley, a former member of the Quorum of Twelve Apostles:

"I've learned a lot from these islanders that I see scattered around here. I see Albert Whaanga down there from New Zealand. I wish he'd teach you people how to rub noses. That's what we do down in New Zealand, you know. We don't really rub. You just press your forehead and your nose against the nose and forehead of the other person.

"It's a wonderful thing. You can always tell when they're keeping the Word of Wisdom down there. All you have to do is walk up and greet them and sniff a little bit, and you've got 'em; you've got 'em!"

(Address to the Brigham Young University Studentbody, Miracles, February 18, 1953, p. 6.)

The following story was told many years ago when people were allowed to smoke in a public building:

Taking her six-year-old daughter Amy with her, Sister Pratt went to a hair salon to have her hair trimmed, washed, and combed. Five hair dryers away from Sister Pratt, a woman was smoking a cigarette.

Not having been around people who smoked, Amy kept staring at this woman. Finally, she hurried and stood in front of this woman and said, "Don't you know that you're not supposed to smoke?"

This woman was quite indignant and responded, "Who says I can't smoke?"

With courage, Amy declared, "Smokey the Bear and Holy the Ghost!"

ABOUT THE COMPILER

Bruce E. Dana is an avid student of the gospel, who served as a missionary in the Northwestern States and Pacific Northwest missions for the Church. He attended Weber State College and Utah State University. Brother Dana has served in a wide variety of Church callings and enjoys teaching the doctrines of the gospel. He is married to Brenda Lamb and is the father of eight children.

Brother Dana is the author of seven published LDS doctrinal books. They are: (1) Mysteries of the Kingdom, (2) Mary, Mother of Jesus, (3) Simon Peter, (4) The Three Nephites and Other Translated beings, (5) Glad Tidings Near Cumorah, (6) The Eternal Father and His Son, and [7] The Apostleship.

After writing the aforementioned doctrinal books, Brother Dana decided to try his hand at a humor book. Accordingly, he has compiled this work.

In his doctrinal works, Brother Dana has often obtained permission to quote from the writings of Elder Bruce R. McConkie, a former member of the Quorum of the Twelve Apostles.

Brother Dana jokingly says, "When I used to say my prayers, the Lord would say, 'I know Bruce R., but who is Bruce E.?'"